Magnetic Faith

A Bold Guide To Creating The
Breakthrough Life You Want God's Way

David Ramos

Copyright © 2019 by David Ramos.

ALL RIGHTS RESERVED.

No part of this publication may be reproduced, distributed, or transmitted in any form or by any means, including photocopying, recording, or other electronic or mechanical methods, without the prior written permission of the publisher, except in the case of brief quotations embodied in critical reviews and certain other noncommercial uses permitted by copyright law. For permission requests, please contact the author through the Contact Form on his website: RamosAuthor.com

All Scripture quotations, unless otherwise indicated, are taken from the Holy Bible, New International Version®, NIV®. Copyright ©1973, 1978, 1984, 2011 by Biblica, Inc.™ Used by permission of Zondervan. All rights reserved worldwide. www.zondervan.com The "NIV" and "New International Version" are trademarks registered in the United States Patent and Trademark Office by Biblica, Inc.™

Your Free Gift!

Congratulations on picking up this book and taking the next steps towards developing a truly Magnetic Faith. As a thank you, I want to send you 3 gifts that will equip and encourage you along your journey.

To claim your gifts simply go to RamosAuthor.com/

Table of Contents

Preface   1

Part 1: Magnetic Identity   2
  The Question   3
  Ask, Seek, Knock   6
  Who Is This Book For?   9
  The Recipe   11
  The Triangle   14
  Something Unseen   19
  The Upside-Down Gospel   22
  Evidence   24
  Who God Says You Are   27
  The 7 Magnetic Identities   30
  Identity 1: You Are Unique   32
  Identity 2: You Are An Heir   35
  Identity 3: You Are New   38
  Identity 4: You Are Free   41
  Identity 5: You Are Destined   44
  Identity 6: You Are Loved   47

Identity 7: You Are Powerful	50
Acceptance And Belief	54
How To Create And Control Your Identity	56
Part 2: Magnetic Mindset	60
What Do We Mean When We Say "Mindset"?	61
The 3 Dimensions of Your Mind	64
A Note on the Accuser	68
Believe Before You Think	71
The 7 Magnetic Beliefs	74
Mindset 1: Growth Over Fixed	75
Mindset 2: Results Over Failure	78
Mindset 3: Abundance Over Scarcity	81
Mindset 4: Tortoise Over Hare	84
Mindset 5: Focus Over Fad	87
Mindset 6: Authenticity Over Acceptance	90
Mindset 7: God Is For You Not Against You	93
Framing	96
How To Create And Control Your Mindset	100
Part 3: Magnetic Habits	105
What It Means To Have Faith	106
Why Faith Is Dead Without Works	109
Transformed Expectations	113

Why Habits (And Not Just Actions) Are The Key	116
Proclamation, Invitation and Evidence	119
The 7 Magnetic Habits	122
Habit 1: Take Your Bible Seriously	124
Habit 2: Pray Like Your Life Depends On It	127
Habit 3: Tithe From A Place Of Authority	130
Habit 4: Give Your Need	133
Habit 5: Altar-Building To Remember	138
Habit 6: Make Room Through Fasting	143
Habit 7: Affirmations of Divine Truth	147
Form Follows Function	149
How to Create and Control Your Habits	152
Part 4: Magnetic Words	157
You Are Already Magnetic	158
The Tree, The Fruit and The Problem	160
4 Rules For Holy Living	166
How Our Words Work	170
Biblical Ammunition For Your Power	173
Breathe	176
The 3 Magnetic Affirmations	178
Affirmation 1: I Am	180
Affirmation 2: I Believe	184
Affirmation 3: I Commit	189

Never Empty	193
How The Three Work Together	195
Moving Beyond Magnetic Words	198
How To Create and Control Your Words	200
Closing	205
Recommended Reading List	207
Magnetic Faith Mantra	209
About The Author	210
More Books by David Ramos	211
I Need Your Help!	213

David Ramos

Preface

Ask and it will be given to you; seek and you will find; knock and the door will be opened to you.

For everyone who asks receives; the one who seeks finds; and to the one who knocks, the door will be opened.

Which of you, if your son asks for bread, will give him a stone?

Or if he asks for a fish, will give him a snake?

If you, then, though you are evil, know how to give good gifts to your children, how much more will your Father in heaven give good gifts to those who ask him!

Matthew 7:7-11

Magnetic Faith

Part 1: Magnetic Identity

How To Tap Into The Power Of Who God Says You Are

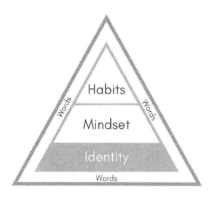

The Question

"In the morning, LORD, you hear my voice; in the morning I lay my requests before you and wait expectantly...Surely, LORD, you bless the righteous."
Psalm 5:3, 12

I want to ask you a question, and I want you to be honest with yourself. No one has to know your answer. You don't have to say it aloud or write it down. All I want you to do is answer it for yourself – truthfully, honestly. You have nothing to hide or apologize for. Okay, here is the question:

What do you want? *order. Spiritual, Financial, Physical, emotional*

What was the first thing that came to mind? *I want to be order healthy, I want to be married, I want a different job, I want my wife to forgive me, I want my business to succeed, I want my brother to be ok, I want to know what to do...*

Now, I want you to think about how you feel about that thing you want.

Do you feel anxious or worried because it feels outside of your control? Do you feel guilty because maybe you're not being content? Do you feel depressed because the situation seems hopeless? Or do you feel happy, excited, and confident <u>because you know, beyond the shadow of a doubt, that what you want is working out, coming to pass, and happening soon?</u>

This last feeling is what Psalm 5 describes when it says that we are to "wait expectantly" on the Lord. This is the mode or attitude God wants us to take on when we lay our requests, or wants, before Him. <u>To be expectant literally means to be filled with excitement at the prospect of what is going to happen.</u>

I have had the pleasure of teaching preschool Sunday school classes for almost 8 years now. Those little humans have easily taught me just as much about God and Scripture as any seminary course or theology book.

One of the most eye-opening parts of working with these children is how bold they are in their requests. I've had kids ask to paint the walls, to teach them how to drive, to make their baby brother disappear, or to buy them a puppy. If it mattered to them, they asked. Boldly, confidently, expectantly. And even when the answer was no, they found a way to ask for something else. Their attitude never changing, never shrinking away.

I've never seen a preschooler condemn themselves for being too selfish, or feel guilty for asking too big. They are excited to be alive, and know that I am there as their teacher because A. I care about them and B. I promise to take care of them. I actually love when they ask me for anything, and you can be sure that anything that is in my power to give them, and good for them, I give them right away. When going through security today, I asked God to hide my small scissors in my bag. I did not get stopped.

An orderly life feels...

- peaceful
- happy
- [free]
- productive

I am walking towards my orderly life.

I keep moving forward towards the orderly, peaceful, life I desire.

I am excited about the life of order I am creating.

Ask, Seek, Knock

These ideas about wants, requests, and little children all came to mind during the year I spent studying a single passage of Scripture: Matthew 7:7-12.

The passage begins with one of the most recognizable lines from the Bible, "*Ask and it will be given to you; seek and you will find; knock and the door will be opened to you.*" I learned a tremendous amount about this passage during my time studying it. But what still strikes me even to this day, even after reading it some 400 times, is how *sure* it is. That if you ask, it *will* be given. And if you seek, you *will* find. And for those who knock, that door *will* open. It was sure in a way my faith and my requests to God had never really been. It was confident and powerful and beautiful. The only thing I could relate it to in my mind was a magnet.

A magnet attracts. That's what it does, attracting is a part of its innate properties. It doesn't have to work hard at attracting, or feel a certain way before it can attract. It just does because that's what it was made to do.

You were made to be a child of God. That was always the intention before sin got in the way. But the problem is that even once we take care of that sin by accepting and proclaiming Jesus as our Savior, the "magnet" part of our faith still seems to be off. So many Christians, so many of us, still struggle with financial lack or health issues or abuse or just general lostness.

Somewhere along the way we've accepted salvation without accepting everything that comes along with it. First and foremost: the ability to ask our Heavenly Father with expectation. Expectation that He will act, that He will give, that He will open.

I decided I wanted that. I wanted my faith to be magnetic: to be sure, confident, and expectant. I wanted my relationship with God to take on a whole new dimension where I truly believed these things I saw in Scripture, and that He would transform every aspect of my life because of them: my finances, my relationships, my health, my career, and more.

The crazy thing is... it worked!

As I began to make these small, Biblically-informed changes to the way I thought, prayed, and acted my life began to change right before my eyes. My health improved, my debts disappeared, doors opened I never could have opened on my own, and my relationship with God flourished.

I want you to pay attention to this idea: my relationship with God flourished most not when I was in lack, fearful and praying small "humble" prayers. Rather, as my life became fuller, my relationship with God became richer.

And this is what I want for you.

I want you to have the most vibrant, intimate, exciting relationship with the God of the universe you can possibly have because that's what we were made for! And I want you to have a life you are ferociously excited to live. A body you are excited to wake up in. A mind you are confident to sit quietly with. A faith that is truly magnetic. Because these too, are what you were made for.

Who Is This Book For?

This book is for Christians who aren't afraid to want. Who aren't afraid to ask big requests of their BIG GOD.

Who understand their time on this earth is limited, so they must make the most of it.

This book is for you if your goal is to learn how to develop a magnetic faith. A faith that is expectant. A faith that gets things done, that improves people's lives, and that furthers the kingdom of God in a tangible way.

This book is for those who are ready for more and not ashamed to admit it. Ready for more abundance, more influence, more responsibility, more peace, and more God moments in their everyday.

This book will shine the light on what has gotten you this far, and give you the tools you need to break through and go further. What got you *here* won't get you *there*. Where *there* is is between you and God. But the method for reaching it is where I fit into the equation.

Equipping you to become the *who* you were called to be is my calling, so that you can accomplish the *what* you were created to do.

If you want that, then keep reading.

The Recipe

"When I discover who I am, I'll be free" – Ralph Ellison

"Guard your heart above all else, for it determines the course of your life." Proverbs 4:23 (NLT)

There's a reason we find it so difficult to change our lives. I'm going to explain to you why, but first I want to tell you a story.

When I worked at the local college, we would have a potluck at the end of each semester. It was a time to celebrate, to de-stress from all the normal work demands, and enjoy some amazing food. This last part was key. We had about a dozen incredible cooks on our staff, so every time we had a potluck the spread they created was unbelievable. The smell would carry through the halls and down the stairs and it wouldn't take long for our small area to fill up with over 40 hungry guests.

Because there were so many good cooks, people would end up sharing recipes with one another. You could glance across the room and almost always catch 2 or 3 people scribbling away. *You said 2 teaspoons...? Oh, that's oregano... I would never have guessed that was in there...!*

One of the recipes I jotted down was an almost-vegetarian lasagna. Everything in the lasagna was made from vegetables (zucchini noodles, veggie toppings, and vegetable only sauce ingredients). Except, the recipe added in 1lb of ground turkey. You could leave it out, of course, if you wanted the authentic vegetarian experience. But most people preferred having a little meat inside to give it some weight.

The next time we had a potluck, I chose to make that recipe. I pulled out my scribbled notes and read line by line to make sure I had bought all the correct ingredients. I cooked it according to the instructions and brought it for lunch that day with a proud smile on my face.

Before long, we dug in and began to eat. Everything was good, but something was off. My lasagna wasn't quite right. The taste was off – not bad – just incorrect. I had some other people taste it and they came to the same conclusion. So I took my plate over to the person I had gotten the recipe from and asked her to tell me what was wrong.

She took a bite and asked, *so what did you put in this again?*

I listed off the ingredients: zucchini for the noodles, Roma tomatoes for the sauce, onions and garlic, spinach with the ricotta, ground turkey for the meat, and...

She stopped me. *Oh, honey, I don't use ground turkey, I use sausage. It's got more of a spice, that's why your flavor is off.*

She knew right away what the problem was and how to fix it. My food was off because my recipe was off. It wouldn't have mattered how many times I cooked that recipe, how well I seasoned it, or how fresh those vegetables were before I cooked them. The recipe was incomplete, incorrect, and therefore my end result would always be lacking.

It's a silly example but it illustrates the next point very well. You trying to change yourself BY YOURSELF is like you trying to correct the taste of an incorrect recipe. Chances are, if you're reading this, you've tried to change some troublesome area of your life before with little success. Maybe you tried to lose weight but gained it all back. Maybe you changed jobs thinking it'd make you happier, only to end up more frustrated. Maybe you started going to a new church, bought new clothes, dumped your loser boyfriend – only to wind up experiencing the same feelings and frustrations that led you to make that change in the first place.

First of all, it's not your fault. Most people have never really thought about the SOURCE of what controls them. Second, you're closer to your goal than you think. The fact that you're reading this book proves that you want something more, that you believe God has something better for you, and that you are willing to do and become who you need to be in order to reach it.

The Triangle

The triangle of what controls you is made up of 4 different parts:

- Your identity or core self
- Your thoughts or mindset
- Your actions or habits
- Your words or speech

The way these parts work together is simple to understand. But the results of understanding how they work can be incredibly powerful.

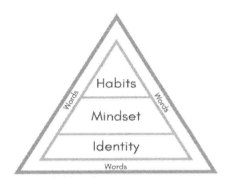

Part 1: Identity

Your identity is the most basic, the most true, and the most influential fact or set of facts you believe about yourself. By basic, I mean this idea is never really up for debate in your mind. You have been X (whatever that is) as long as you can remember, and it's just a part of your most elementary makeup. This could be physical, emotional, mental, relational, or any number of things. When you think about yourself, these are the first ideas that come to mind. For example: *I'm David, a Hispanic male, married, Christian, etc.*

When I say true, I mean that we believe these things about ourselves for some reason, whether or not they are accurate. For example, I believe I am smart because of how I performed in school. But if I went to school with only geniuses and saw that I wasn't *as smart* as them, then I probably would have associated my identity with being less smart or even dumb.

Now, it wouldn't have been true – but I used the evidence I had to reach a conclusion that made sense to me. We've done this in all sorts of ways and these identity facts we believe have had all sorts of positive and negative effects in our lives. This is what I mean by influential. Your decisions are a result of numerous factors. But at the deepest level, they are a direct result of what you believe to be true about yourself.

I identify as being a writer. That identity shapes everything else in my life – the thoughts I think, the actions I take, and the words I speak. I do not identify as being a great dancer, and so the thoughts, actions, and words that follow are also impacted. Everything flows from identity, and if you can control this piece – you can control your entire life.

Part 2: Mindset

The next part is your mindset or thought-life. This is one that has received a lot of attention in both the Christian and non-Christian spheres, and for good reason. It's important! Your thoughts control more than you can possibly imagine. They not only impact how you feel and what you do, but they can impact and influence the world around you. They can make you physically sick or help you become healthy. They can drive you to depression or give you superhuman energy. They can move you to take enormous risks or keep you handcuffed to mediocrity.

The thing about thoughts is that we don't always know where they come from, and sometimes when we try to control them it's like trying to run into the middle of a highway and start directing traffic. Our brains work like roadways, and the roads that get traveled most often expand to allow more and more traffic through. So when we try to change our thoughts, it really is like trying to perform mental construction – to shut down destructive roadways and expand the areas we want to grow.

Your mind is a tool, a battlefield, and a garden. If you can get it on your side, anything is possible.

Part 3: Habits

The third part of the triangle is habits or actions. This part is where we spend the most time, money and energy trying to change. Why? Because this is the piece of the puzzle we can clearly see. We can see ourselves getting heavier, or being lazy on the couch, or not keeping our commitments. Because we can see these "bad" actions or habits, we begin to feel a certain way. We feel negative or guilty or overwhelmed or frustrated, and those feelings temporarily move us to a different action.

The problem is, feelings change. And when they do, our actions change with them. It's when we stop feeling guilty or frustrated that we revert back to our unhelpful habits. They become our safe-space, our default. But the good news is, it's possible to change our default. More than that, it's possible to develop a life that is built upon actions that are uninfluenced by our feelings.

That means when things get difficult, we will still choose to do what is right. When the hard thing stares us in the face and tries to convince us to back down, we won't. The habits we now choose are built on something stronger. Something indestructible and unrelenting. And because of that, we can now build a life that is also indestructible and unrelenting.

"...it's possible to develop a life that is built upon actions that are uninfluenced by our feelings."

Part 4: Words

Last but not least, the building blocks of the triangle itself: our words. In Proverbs 18:21 we learn that the "tongue has the power of life and death."

I want you to take a minute and think about things in our current society that have the "power of life and death." Here is what comes to my mind: guns, court judges, powerful medications, huge bodies of water. In one way, all of these things have the power to protect and to improve the quality of one's life. In another way, any one of these can take away life in an instant. These have incredible power which is why there are rules governing how they work: who can have a gun, who can become a judge, who can access and prescribe medications, and who can guard these bodies of water.

God says in His Word that our tongues are just as powerful, meaning they are just as able to protect as they are to harm. Our words can improve the quality of our life or they can destroy it. We need to take our words seriously. Our current life is a product of our words. If we want something different in any area of our life, then we must harness the power of our words to get there.

Something Unseen

"We know what we are, but not what we may be." –
William Shakespeare

In 2010, I begin the practice of choosing one passage of Scripture to study for an entire year. I've done it every year since then, and it has easily been one of the most important parts of my spiritual growth. The passage that started it all was Colossians 3:1-17.

In Colossians, Paul talks about incredible, lofty subjects like the supremacy of God and the immense freedom we have in Christ. Over and over again, he pushes the reader to see themselves as different, as new. He wants his brothers and sisters in Christ to understand the *advantage* they have because of their new status.

All of this comes to a climax in chapter 3. This is where, in my opinion, Paul delivers one of the most well-crafted explanations of what it means to be Christian in the entire Bible. Furthermore, this passage provided the framework for my entire "triangle of what controls you" concept.

ust like us. Actually, more like us than
 imagine. He had bad habits. He said
etted. His mind entertained wrong
is basically an extended rant about
.... it is to become the person God is calling us
.. be. But Paul did not give up. He understood that if something wasn't working properly, then there had to be another force at work – something underneath, something deeper, something unseen. It was this thinking that led him to write Colossians 3.

"Since, then, you have been raised with Christ, set your hearts on things above, where Christ is, seated at the right hand of God. Set your minds on things above, not on earthly things. For you died, and your life is now hidden with Christ in God." Colossians 3:1-3

Identity can be a hard thing to talk about because it seems so intangible. It's hard for us to fully define our identity, let alone mold it and shape it into what we want. But identity is the crux of everything you want. It's the foundation for a renewed mind, the basis for actions that will make you proud, and the source for words that will transform your life.

Paul got this idea, which is why he begins the passage by telling his readers – *you are different now*. Your heart, the core of your being, your identity, has been *raised* with Christ. What does this mean? Paul goes on to help us understand, "for you died, and your life is now hidden...".

What Paul is saying is that the moment you accept and acknowledge Jesus as your Lord, something shifts, both in this realm and in the realm of the unseen – the layer that is underneath which controls everything. Just as Jesus rose from the dead and became something new, but still himself, the same thing is happening to you.

In a sense, something inside of you dies. Paul calls it the old self or sin or the law. The important piece is, the new you is defined by freedom. The new you is defined by glory. The new you is alive in the truest sense of the word.

It's because of this new *aliveness* that other changes can begin to happen: setting your mind on things above (v.2) (aka thinking differently), putting to death your earthly nature (v.5) (aka ending your destructive habits and replacing them with productive actions), and letting the message of Christ transform you (v.16) (aka speaking different words).

All of it begins with and rests on the identity shift. The acknowledgment that we are who and what Jesus says we are. Only when God's view of you becomes your view of you can all of the other changes begin to take root.

Trying to change your words, actions, and mindset without changing your identity is like trying to season a rotten piece of meat. You might be able to make it look or smell more appealing, but at the end of the day, it's still bad for you.

The Upside-Down Gospel

This is the point Paul drives home. Everything we want to have, do and become relies on our accepting and acknowledging who we are in, through, and because of Christ. The *new self* is not something we work towards, but that we work from.

We don't work on our words, actions, and thoughts so that we can become who Jesus says we can be. That would be the logical way to go about this. But the essence of the Gospel is that God does things backward, or more appropriately, upside-down. The first are last, the least are greatest, the humble are exalted, and the prodigal sons are accepted not because of what they've done but purely on the basis of who they are.

Everything that follows in this book rests on this premise: we are already everything God wants us to be.

You will never be more loved by God than you are in this very moment. Right now, just as you are, God is as proud of you as He will ever be.

Jesus understood this.

In Matthew 3, the writer records the beginning of Jesus' ministry. John the Baptist meets Jesus at the Jordan river and baptizes him. As soon as Jesus comes out of the water, God speaks from the heavens, "This is my Son, whom I love; with him I am well pleased" (Mathew 3:17).

Before a single miracle.

Before a single sermon.

Before the cross.

God booms down from the heavens to tell His son, *hey, I'm super proud of you.* Jesus' entire ministry was founded on this truth: our identity is what drives everything about us. Jesus worked from a place of acceptance. That is what gave him his power and authority and freedom.

If this is the pattern Jesus used for his ministry, how much more should this be the pattern we adopt for our lives?

Evidence

We've talked about changing or reclaiming our God-given identity. But I think it's important we ask a question before we get too much further. How did our identity get off track in the first place? How did we stray and become mis-molded into something we were never meant to be?

It comes down to two words: evidence and conclusion.

When my brother and I were too young for school, our grandma used to babysit us along with the two kids next door: a girl, who is my brother's age, and her younger brother. I remember one day we decided to have a little pre-birthday party for my brother. Grandma baked some cupcakes and all of us kids got to decorate them with frosting and sprinkles. I can only imagine the mess it must have been!

Since it was my brother's birthday, grandma lit a single candle atop his cupcake so that we could sing to him before he ate it. There we were, my brother sitting in front of his cupcake, me on one side, the girl his age on the other, when the youngest child in my grandma's arms reached his little hand directly into the bright, dancing flame.

He yanked his hand back immediately, almost too surprised to cry. But after a second of being stunned, he let out a wail like you wouldn't believe. The interesting part is what happened next. The small child wouldn't eat his cupcake. In fact, he wouldn't even go near it. Every time we tried to offer it to him, he began to cry.

He avoided cupcakes at the next birthday and the one after that. It took nearly an entire year before he realized the pain he felt was not caused by the cupcake, but by the candle that was on top. The conclusion or interpretation he reached was incorrect because his evidence was incomplete: "if I touch this dessert, I will experience pain." It took time and the presentation of different, better evidence, to prove to him that cupcakes were safe.

You and I work the same way.

The identities we claim are built upon the evidence life presents to us and the conclusions we consciously or unconsciously accept to be true.

I was a heavier kid growing up, and that physical factor shaped aspects of my identity. Because I was big and had trouble running, I believed that I could never be athletic. The evidence I saw around me, which was reinforced by what others said, is what I used to create a conclusion that made sense.

We do this in all sorts of ways and in all areas of our lives. We take in evidence about our relationships, health, finances, abilities, etc. and reach "logical" conclusions about who we are and where we fit in the world.

The problem is, most of the evidence around us is incomplete! Most people around us are not living their best life or doing the work necessary to become the best versions of themselves. So instead of raw, neutral evidence what we actually pick up is biased limitations. We hear and see the limitations others put on themselves, and rather than questioning whether or not they are accurate or necessary, we instead learn how to adopt their limitations as our own.

We limit what we can do, where we can go, what we can think – over and over again, building a box around our lives. And by default, we create our identity not from a place of possibility, but from a place of limitation. We define who we are not by what we can be, but by what we are not.

I'm not that smart... I'm not athletic... My family isn't rich... No one I know has started a business...

So then, if this is how we got to where we are: by using incomplete evidence to produce limiting conclusions. The way forward is to do the opposite. To present you with complete, true, powerful, divine evidence for who you really are so that, equipped with this new information, you can produce different, empowering, possibility-infused conclusions.

Who God Says You Are

"400 trillion to 1, those are the odds of becoming a human being." – Gary Vaynerchuk

Do you know who you are? Do you know what God says about you in His Word?

Did you know that you were made to "sparkle...like jewels in a crown"? (Zechariah 9:16)

That you were created to be crowned – with glory and honor (Hebrews 2). When God looks at you He says, *I have put everything under your feet.*

Did you know that you, a mortal being, would one day be called upon to "judge angels" (1 Corinthians 6:3)

You are extraordinary!

You were made on purpose (Psalm 139). Every hair on your head was placed there with care. God calculated your weight, brushed on your color, gave you that dimple or birthmark and said *Yes, this is exactly what I want! Perfect.*

He thinks you're perfect (Psalm 139:14).

He's crazier about you and thinks about you more often than you thought about your first crush.

He's more excited than a parent on Christmas morning, just before the kids begin to open their presents because he knows all the good things he has for us. (Matthew 7:11)

God literally bent and broke the rules of the created universe to make a way for you and Him to be together. He is that in love with you... that crazy about you... You are that valuable to him.

You are chosen. (Colossians 3:12)

You are enough, whole, complete. (Colossians 2:10)

You are free – in every way you understand that word to mean, and in a million ways you've yet to discover. (Galatians 5:1)

You are heir to the very kingdom of heaven, and to the world itself. (Romans 8:17)

You are both God's child (the apple of his eye) and God's friend (the one he longs to be with). (John 1:12, 15:15)

You lack nothing (Philippians 4:19): not materials, not courage, not worth, not friends or time or anything you could possibly need to be and do what God has for you in this very moment.

You are powerful (Luke 10:17-19) and you are loved (John 3:16). So very, very loved.

You need to hear these things over and over again until they seep into the fabric of your soul and become non-negotiable. As we continue through the 4 parts of Magnetic Faith, you'll learn exactly how to make this happen. But for now, our next step is to focus in on some of these truths.

What I shared with you above is just a fraction of what God's Word says about you. I hope from just that small sample you are beginning to get a sense of how much of an identity shift needs to occur inside all of us.

Don't let your familiarity with any of those phrases subtract from their truth and power in your life. Quite literally, the fate of the world rests upon you believing what God says about you. We were not meant to sit and merely watch the story of the world unfold. We were created to shape it, to play a role in the divine drama that nobody else could ever play.

In my own journey of faith and purpose, seven of these truths have stood out more than all the rest. Seven statements that, I believe, are the foundation upon which all of the other truths and promises are built. If you can get these, if you can allow this new evidence to reshape your conclusion and redefine your identity – your life will literally transform from the inside out.

The 7 Magnetic Identities

Living the life you desire to have, that you were created to live, begins with accepting the truth about who you are. Everything in your life is a product of the identity you have accepted to be true about yourself: the quality of your relationships, the financial level you have reached, the content of your thoughts. Even the way you organize your time and physical spaces are an outworking of your accepted identity.

This means that every change you want to make in your life must begin at the identity level. The seen is merely a product of the unseen.

Some of these 7 identity truths will resonate more than others. Perhaps you already believe a few of them. Perhaps there is one you fear you might never be able to fully believe.

I want you to temporarily put all of these thoughts aside for the next few minutes. For now, I want you to imagine that you were hired into a new role at Fulfilled Inc. It's your first day and at orientation, they hand you a document which lists your job duties. Like any new job, you might feel a little overwhelmed at first because you don't know how to do some of these things yet.

The following 7 truths are not only opportunities God wants you to take full advantage of; they are also duties. In order for you to become the *who* you were meant to be, and do the *what* you were created to do, you have to step into these roles. They must move from something you can be, to something you must be because they lay the foundation for everything else.

Identity 1: You Are Unique

Evidence: *Psalm 139:14; Ephesians 2:10; Matthew 10:30*

"Still, God, you are our Father. We're the clay and you're our potter: All of us are what you made us." Isaiah 64:8 (MSG)

Several years ago, my brother and I started collecting small vinyl figurines of our favorite video game characters. It's a simple way we get to stay connected to each other as well as to our childhood selves.

As we've become more knowledgeable collectors, we've developed an eye for what makes one piece more valuable than another. A slight variation in color or size can triple the value of a piece. And by far, the most value-increasing attribute is "limited production."

When there were only 50 or 100 of a certain collectible ever produced – the value of each one of those items can be astronomical. For example, one piece we picked up was a limited run of 50. We bought the piece for the standard price of $12 when it was released and within 2 years, it is now worth over $1,400.

But that is pocket change compared to the holy grails of the collecting community: one-of-a-kinds. These are pieces created by the original artist either as a prototype or for a special event. These items draw in awe and praise and fetch prices in the tens of thousands of dollars. Why? Because once you have one of these, your collection is unlike any other. It can't be copied or reproduced. It stands out, apart, and above because its value rests on its uniqueness.

You, reading this, are a one-of-a-kind. Created by the original artist. Unable to be copied or reproduced. Invaluable.

Sometimes we get confused about our uniqueness because we let our identity get distracted or associated with things that aren't really us. You might think *I'm not the only 29-year-old manager* or *I'm not the only single mom with 2 kids who works 3 jobs* or *I'm definitely not the only John Smith*.

That's because you are MORE than your job, MORE than your relationships and family, and MORE than your name. You are unique. You are MORE than the sum of the pieces that make you up.

No one on earth has ever thought exactly like you, lived through the same situations in the same order, and came out the other end with the same dreams, passions, and desires. Your uniqueness makes you indispensable.

You've probably heard this analogy before, but it's such a clear example of why being unique matters! Imagine building a puzzle, spending hours working to get the outline structured so you can begin filling in the center, working to match colors and shapes, until – at last – you're down to the final piece. But as you look across the table, there are no more pieces. You open the puzzle box to check you didn't leave it in there by mistake, no luck. You get down on the floor, crawling around, searching for this missing piece. You check your pockets and clothes. You put your eye level with the table to see if maybe the piece is hiding atop or underneath the puzzle itself. Still nothing.

Why do you search so hard for this single piece? Because the puzzle will remain incomplete without it. It may not have seemed as important as a corner piece. But, in the grand scheme of things – it's the most important piece on the board because it's irreplaceable. You can't move things around and try to make another piece fill its spot. It'll never fit quite right, and then that will just cause another gap somewhere else in the puzzle. It has to be that piece, that exact color, shape, and size for it to work.

You are no less important. Nothing about you is a mistake. Everything about you makes you the exact fit for the picture God is creating. There is no waste in God's design. We need you just as you are.

Identity 2: You Are An Heir

Evidence: *Romans 8:17; 1 Peter 1:4; Revelation 21:7*

"The Spirit himself testifies with our spirit that we are God's children. Now if we are children, then we are heirs…" Romans 8:16, 17a

"You try living for 15 years thinking that you're one person, and then in five minutes, you find out you're a princess. Just in case I wasn't enough of a freak already, let's add a tiara!"
– Mia in The Princess Diaries

Mia had no idea who she really was. She grew up living in a context that told her she was average at best and an ugly, unpopular loser at worst. These ideas shaped her. They shaped what she thought she could accomplish, who she thought she could date, and how her life, as a whole, would ultimately look.

It took an outsider (Queen Renaldi, Mia's grandmother) to reveal to her (and convince her) about her true identity. Once Mia accepted it to be true – the work of transformation began. Mia began learning all of the duties and formalities that came with her new self. But it took some time before she could truly understand all of the benefits that came with being the princess.

I've found that Christians are very similar.

We accept Jesus as our Lord and Savior and even learn to identify as being a part of God's family. Yet, we neglect to investigate what the rewards and benefits of this new position truly are! Yes, there are rewards in the life to come, but there are also promised rewards for HERE and for NOW.

> Yet I am confident I will see the LORD's goodness while I am here in the land of the living. Psalm 27:13

Being an heir rearranges your place in the divine order of the universe. You become the head and not the tail, the lender and not the borrower, the one who acts and speaks and thinks from a place of abundance, a place of acceptance, a place of power.

I want you to read the next line slowly:

> God owns everything. Everything He has is ours. (Luke 15:31)

Every mountain. Every animal. Every body of water.

Every house you want to buy. Every job you're praying to get. Every single thing. It may be guarded by a human steward, but it ultimately belongs to God. And as His heir, whatever it is, whatever we desire no matter how big, is ultimately ours as well.

Woah David, what about...

Here's where part of me wanted to write a short paragraph about limits. The practical, logical, "good Christian" part of me wanted to encourage you to be humble. Because what would happen if Christians actually prayed like heirs? Wouldn't that be greedy? If everyone prayed for everything, wouldn't that be too much? I decided against it because I believe it is always better to stray on the side of asking God for too much, rather than too little.

The size of your prayers reflects the size of your God. For you to properly accept your role as an heir also requires you to accept the incomprehensible size of your God. Believing that you can have anything begins by believing that God already has everything.

Identity 3: You Are New

Evidence: *Isaiah 43:18-19; Ephesians 4:24; Ezekiel 36:26*

"Therefore, if anyone is in Christ, the new creation has come: The old has gone, the new is here!" 2 Corinthians 5:17

One summer, my wife and I got serious about our health. We drastically changed our diet: removed sugar, increased our vegetables, opted for organic when we could, and paid close attention to everything we allowed into our bodies. That summer we both lost 20+ pounds and felt amazing.

One side effect of losing that much weight is that our clothes began to fit differently, and some of them no longer fit at all. I had one pair of pants in particular which were my favorite. They had been exactly the right size and length and felt great. They gave me confidence when I wore them, like they were my second skin. But after my weight loss, they looked strange. The waste bunched up under the belt, also causing the pants to look longer than they were. They were no longer comfortable or confidence-boosting. They became a chore to wear because they didn't fit right, so I eventually got rid of them and bought a new pair of pants which fit correctly.

This is how Colossians 3 talks about our new self. That we have to "put it on" like a pair of great-fitting pants. But in order to do that, we first have to take off the old self – the things which no longer fit. This is where forgiveness comes in.

Forgiveness is like a healthy diet for the soul. It enables us to shed the unnecessary, unhelpful weight we've been carrying around so that we can put on the *new self* God intended. If you are in Christ, then you are forgiven of shame, forgiven of guilt, forgiven of mistakes. You're lighter now. Your whole shape has changed and now you need to put on the clothes that fit: power, compassion, discipline, patience, peace, and love (Colossians 3:12-14).

Your new self looks different because your new self *is* different.

The most powerful part (and what I think is the most exciting part) of being new is that newness is never stationary. Once you understand yourself to be new, you enter an ever-increasing cycle of newness. Paul calls it a transformation "from one degree of glory to another" (2 Corinthians 3:18 ESV).

Newness begets more newness.

In our health journey, my wife and I didn't begin with all the pieces in place. We began with healthier snacks, which eventually led to healthier meals. Those healthier meals gave us the energy to begin incorporating exercise. Exercise gave us the hunger and desire for even cleaner eating, which led to more energy. And because we felt so good, we could do more – like cleaning our apartment more often. Having a cleaner apartment made us want to invite people over more often. Which, in turn, led to more transformation in other areas of our lives.

One drop of newness has the power to transform your entire life if you let it. This is what God wants you to get: His newness isn't just for your spiritual health, it's for every area of your life. He wants you to be lightened by your new identity so that you can put on the proper fitting garments, so that you are equipped to fulfill the extraordinary life He has called you to, so that you can enjoy His incredible blessings...and on and on!

Newness never stops renewing. It never stops giving and building and transforming and opening. The newness God desires for all creation requires you.

Identity 4: You Are Free

Evidence: *John 8:36; Psalm 119:45; 2 Corinthians 3:17*

"It is for freedom that Christ has set us free. Stand firm, then, and do not let yourselves be burdened again by a yoke of slavery." Galatians 5:1

Freedom lies in being bold. – Robert Frost

A practice I like to do with my students is when we come across a familiar word, we dive into the etymology, or origin, of the word to discover the true depth of its meaning. Free or freedom is a word we've all been exposed to at least a million times in our lives. Because of that, it comes with various meanings and preconceptions which may or may not be helpful. I want to take a minute to uncover its origin so that you can know what it is you are stepping into.

We'll begin with "freedom." Freedom is made up of two parts: "free" an adjective and "-dom" a suffix. At first, we can see that the word freedom means *power, deliverance, exemption from control.*[i]

If we take a step deeper, we learn that "dom", at its core, means law or judgment. "Free" has multiple, useful ideas I want to share. First, the origin of free crisscrosses with these words: loved, joyful, noble, friend. There's an embedded emotional and relational meaning to the word "free." At another level down, we learn that "free" also has these physical ideas: clear of obstruction, wild, unrestrained in movement.[ii]

Now let's bring it all together. When God calls you free (which He has), He is saying:

My child, the chains upon your life have been broken. You are no longer bound by those things that attempted to make you a slave or make you small or make you afraid. I am giving you power today to walk in this freedom. Look at your arms, there are no chains! Look at your hands, they are yours to use as you see fit. Look at your legs and your feet, they are free to move about, to explore the beauty I created for you. Now that you are free my child, you can experience my love the way you were always meant to. My love does not close doors. When my love shapes you, it does not try to put you in a box. Rather, my love is like a chisel – it removes everything that will slow you down and hold you back. You are free my child, go and use this freedom.

I still remember the first time someone explained to me that God's freedom was both a *freedom from* and a *freedom for*. You see, one half of the definition deals with deliverance. There are things we no longer have to deal with or answer to once we accept and proclaim God's freedom: sin, lack, lies, worldly constraints, and destructive habits to name a few. Just as forgiveness can make us "light," freedom makes us lighter. This is necessary for the second half of the definition to take effect. Freedom for: for power, abundance, truth, divine favor, productive lives, blossoming relationships, mountain-moving work, and miracle-producing actions.

I need you to understand this: God's sense of freedom is not opening the cage of sin so that you can wander into the cage of righteousness.

God's version of freedom for you is not a cage or a box or a set of rules. It's an open field, a blank page. You can go in any direction, you can paint with any color. You can become the truest version of yourself. You can be unapologetically bold. You can literally do and have and be anything for God's glory!

What would your life look like if you saw yourself as completely "unrestrained in movement"? Unrestrained by your past, by finances, by self-imposed limitations? This freedom God has for you is real, and it is yours for the taking.

Identity 5: You Are Destined

Evidence: *Romans 8:28; Isaiah 46:10; Jeremiah 1:5*

"God: I know what I'm doing. I have it all planned out—plans to take care of you, not abandon you, plans to give you the future you hope for." Jeremiah 29:11b (MSG)

> Does the walker choose the path, or the path the walker? – Garth Nix

I LOVE writing on the subjects of calling and purpose. They light me up because I see them as an essential part of how God is remaking all creation for His glory. However, I think we, as Christians, have lost sight of the weight of these subjects.

You see, there seems to be a *choice* when it comes to calling, or an *option* when talking about purpose. The most common question I receive is "how do I know if I'm following my purpose?" There's a sense that we can deny or avoid or miss the thing God has for us to do.

In Lord of the Rings, we see Frodo stumble into a story he never intended to be a part of. He didn't know his uncle possessed one of the most powerful rings, or that it would eventually fall to him to destroy it and save the world. They didn't have a class on that sort of thing in hobbit-school. He tried to get out of it at first, but events kept pulling him back in and confirming that he was the only one who could do it. This thing was weightier, more unrelenting than just a nagging feeling. This was his fate, his destiny. And it wasn't going anywhere until he faced it.

You too are destined.

I like to use this word because there's a finality to it. A decisive factor, cutting off every other distracting option. Destiny eliminates doubt. We don't hear people talking about missing or avoiding their destiny. The word means it's assured, planned, guaranteed.

When God created you, he also destined you. Destined you for greatness, for love, for more – all since you were born. It's not an *if* these things will happen, but a *when*. Destiny is the current of God's will upon creation. It's non-negotiable, and it's working for your good.

Destiny works hand in hand with freedom. What will bring you the most joy, and God the most glory, is sealed in unbreakable stone. But the *how* of accomplishing it, the winding path you take to get there, is completely up to you.

All of this reminds us that no matter where we may be at this moment, we are right on track. You have not sent God into frizzy by your life detours. God has accounted for all of it, and He has secured your destiny regardless. You are sitting where you need to sit, reading what you need to read, and becoming the person you need to be in order to end up exactly where God destined you to reach.

Remember, God knows what He is doing.

Identity 6: You Are Loved

Evidence: *Jeremiah 31:3; 1 John 3:1a; Romans 5:8*

"How great is the love the Father has lavished on us, that we should be called children of God!" 1 John 3:1

Love is worth everything. Everything. – Nicola Yoon

I remember the day I proposed to my wife like it was yesterday. It was July 4, 2014, and I had planned out the entire day for us. I spent all morning making sure everything was ready. At lunchtime, I picked her up from her house and brought her back to mine so I could cook her a quick lunch (she's in love with pasta!). Then, around 3 pm we headed to the dock just outside the city to board a boat called *The Goodtimes*. This boat would take us out onto the water, serve us a beautiful dinner, then park us at the best place to see fireworks in the entire city. As the fireworks began to light up the sky above us, I pulled out the ring I had been anxiously hiding in my pants pocket, got down on one knee, and asked her to marry me. She said yes, and thus began one of the greatest lessons in love.

I love my wife with all my heart. I would do anything to protect her. I always try to think about how I can surprise her or take care of her. I can completely be myself around her – the good and the bad, and she loves me all the same. I trust her and she trusts me. We work for each other's good, support each other's dreams, and push each other to become the best version of ourselves possible.

Loving her makes me a better man. It holds me to a higher standard. Knowing that I am loved gives me a foundation to grow, risk, and build. Because I know that at the end of the day her love isn't going anywhere.

All of this is merely a shadow of God's love for us.

God would do anything to protect you. He thinks about how to surprise you and make you smile. He desires for your truest self to come alive because that's who He created you to be. You can trust Him with even the scariest parts, and He won't let you down. He has your best interest in mind, and the power to make the best come to pass.

He wants you to be better, not so that He can love you more, but so that more of His love can reach you. His love is what gives your soul a home and your body life and your mind hope. His love makes a way where there wasn't one and holds your hands as He walks you across into greener pastures. Love equips, empowers, opens, motivates, transforms, and calms. His love is everything you want but chased other things to get. It's more potent than the satisfaction of power. It's more enticing than sex. It's more enduring than the healthiest marriage.

His love is everything…everything. And all of it is already yours.

You will never be more loved by God than you are at this very moment.

The reason you are here, that you exist, and that you can read this is because you are loved. God's love molded you. It surrounds you and wants to increasingly make its home in you. The only difficult thing about God's love is believing it's real. God's love requires that we understand some human love so that we have some context to build upon. But oh, does it have so much more to give! And it requires so much less!

God loves you without question, without restraint, and without justification. He does not love you *because* or *despite* who you are. He loves all of you, all the time, all the way. His love never fails.

Identity 7: You Are Powerful

Evidence: *Philippians 4:13; Acts 1:8; 1 Corinthians 4:20*

"Very truly I tell you, whoever believes in me will do the works I have been doing, and they will do even greater things than these..." John 14:12a

"The measure of a man is what he does with power." — Plato

What comes to mind when I say the word *power*? For me, it was the first time I saw Zydrunas Savickas (aka Big Z) complete the Atlas Stones event. I was flicking through channels when I saw the World's Strongest Man competition come on the screen. I heard about this competition before but never saw it. I thought it might be cool to see a few insanely strong men push some weight around, but I never thought this one scene would redefine my definition of power.

In order to complete the Atlas Stones, each competitor has to lift 5 stones, each weighing between 220lbs and 350lbs, onto platforms 4 to 5 feet off the ground. The first man went up and lifted the first stone with ease. On the next, you could see that he was really struggling – but after some deep breaths, he heaved it up. On the third, he gave it everything he could, you could see the veins like snakes popping from his neck. But ultimately, he dropped it on the ground and raised his hands up in surrender. The second man completed the first 3 stones but failed on the fourth. The third man did the same. But then, it was Big Z's turn.

Big Z towered over those stones with his 6 ft 3 in and 400lb frame. He had an attitude about him that made everything and everyone else seem smaller. Not in a cocky way either. The only way I could describe it is that he knew his own power; and in this competition, he knew he was powerful enough to win. As the timer started, Big Z squatted down and picked up the first stone like it was a grocery basket. Then the second, and the third, and the fourth – done. Was this guy even human?

When it came to the fifth – the stone no other competitor had even reached yet – you could see his face grow a little redder, and the lift took maybe 3 seconds longer, but then it was done. He placed that 350lb stone atop the platform, gave it a pat, and walked towards his tent. There was a minute, before the cheering, when everyone was silent. What had just happened? Three of the strongest men in the world hadn't even been able to complete the challenge. And yet here was this man, this force, who seemed to be competing at an entirely different level. This became the mental image I think of when I think of the word *power*.

The Bible tells us that God has given us a "spirit of power" (2 Timothy 1:7). So what does that actually look like in our everyday lives? Does it mean we can lift heavy stones or win strength competitions? Does it just apply to the spiritual realm?

When you think of power, I want you to think of Big Z and how he both approached and completed the challenge. Power gave him the confidence to compete. He took stock of what was possible, he measured the difficulty, and approached it as though he has already won. Being in Christ gives us this same power.

Every difficulty or challenge has been placed under our feet already. Even the ones you are still struggling through; even the ones you have yet to encounter. Power changes our approach. If we believe that we have already overcome, that we are victorious, that our God is exceedingly able, and that we already have everything we need to win the day – that places us in a position of power. And then from that secure place, we can approach every challenge with a power that will stop onlookers in their tracks.

Power, in its simplest definition, is the capacity to do. When God looks at us, He says "I have given you the capacity to accomplish everything that I have for you." When Jesus looks at you, He says "I have given you the capacity to do *greater things* than me." The God-man who fed thousands, calmed storms, drove out demons, and raised the dead is telling you, *you will do greater things than these*.

This is why the enemy works so hard to keep you from accepting your power identity. If he can keep you stuck, keep you distracted by stupid sins, keep you feeling defeated and incapable, that is the only way he has a chance of keeping you down. Because if you could catch even a glimpse of your true potential, of your power, of your capacity to shape the very essence of your life and the world around you, he wouldn't stand a chance.

God has called you powerful. He made you capable. The power you need for that challenge, today, is already entirely yours.

Acceptance And Belief

In the movie series *Fast and Furious*, (spoiler alert) one of the main characters, Letty Ortiz, ends up losing her memory as the result of a car wreck. The audience believes she is dead for years before they find out the truth when she shows up with a team of international criminals and attacks her previous family.

Letty lost herself, she lost her identity. She no longer knew what she could hold on to or believe as true. She needed help. Since her internal bearings were off, she needed an external one to set her straight, to help her see once again who she truly was. Dominic Toretto, her life-long love, was the man for the job.

Letty: "That girl you remember, it's not me."

Dominic: "Not from what I just saw. Like it or not, you're still the same girl."

Dominic knew who she was, even when she didn't. After this conversation, Letty switches sides. She joins her old team. Although she is still unsure, she takes the risk towards becoming her true self again because she trusts the one leading her.

God wants to do the same for you.

He wants to break into your false sense of the self, to unravel the lies you have believed, and shine his truth into the crevices of your soul so that every centimeter of your being can be renewed by the truth he has spoken over your life.

One of the first things Dominic did to convince Letty of her true identity was present her with evidence. He showed her pictures of her former life, told her how she had gotten the scars on her body, and gave her her favorite necklace. Piece by piece, he tried to prove to her who she really was. Over time, it began to work – but only because she opened herself up to it. She began to let herself accept the evidence and believe that this whole other life could be true. That this whole other identity could be hers.

This is where a key truth comes in: You can accept your identity before you completely believe it.

In the next part, Magnetic Mindset, we will tackle the tricky subject of beliefs and our thought-life. But that part can only work if this part has begun to take root.

I have done what I can to show you who you really are. I've shown you that you are unique, an heir, new, free, destined, loved, and powerful. I've given you evidence, God's own words in Scripture, to support each one of these claims. But the next part is up to you. You have to be the one to accept these truths. And as you do, you will invite the transformative blessings of God into every area of your life.

How To Create And Control Your Identity

As we close this first section, I know some of you will want to jump right in and start taking action towards reclaiming your identity, and with it, the life you're meant to live. Below are a few guidelines for what to do next.

1. **Keep Reading.** I promise this one is not a cop-out! I want you to understand that the *Magnetic Faith* concept relies on the full triangle – all four parts – and how they interact. Yes, you can start to make serious, felt change in your life by concentrating on the identity portion, but it will only take you so far. You need to understand how your identity plays itself out, and how to transform it from multiple angles, with multiple strategies. That is why my first advice is to continue on to the Magnetic Mindset portion. I promise, the practical steps will come and they will all fit together beautifully!

2. **Memorize These Truths.** I understand for some of you, this section might hit you particularly hard. Or perhaps the Holy Spirit has spoken to you in a special way about one of the identities we covered. If that is the case, then my next piece of advice would be to commit the "evidence" Scriptures to memory. Memorization is a strategy we'll cover in the sections to come, but here you can use it to consistently present yourself with uplifting, Biblical evidence for who you truly are. My suggestion would be to focus on one of the seven identities and over a few weeks, work on memorizing each of the evidence Scriptures related to that specific identity. Once you feel you have a good grasp of that concept, go ahead and move on to the next one. Then continue doing so until you feel ready to engage the Magnetic Mindset portion.

3. **Recognize False Identities.** I have found it helpful, both in my own life, as well as in the lives of my students, to spend time calling out the false identities we have lived with. The easiest way to do this is to pick a specific moment, usually something that has happened within the last 6-8 months, that left you feeling disappointed, or turned out differently than you had hoped. Now, examine that situation and jot down what identities led you to that situation in the first place; and what identities did that result

reinforce? Afterward, look at the seven identities covered in this book and decide which ones could have either prevented or positively changed that situation if you had been living accordingly. This exercise is an excellent way to develop your awareness of false identities – because that is the first step to replacing them!

4. **Write Your Wants.** The last exercise is always a favorite. It's also incredibly powerful when used correctly. First, write down (in detail) the life you desire to live. If you live in a house, where is it? What color is it? How many bathrooms does it have? If you work – do you do so from home? Or from a beautiful building downtown? Are you married? A parent? How do you spend your downtime? What are you known for? How do you feel – about everything? About God? Use as much space as you want to describe the things hidden in your heart. Remember, they are there for a reason.

The second step is to align these wants with the seven identities covered above. How does being unique enable your desires? How does being destined allow for the dream to become reality? How does your freedom fit into this new life? Do this for each of the identities. Try to make sure no piece of your dream life is left out. If it doesn't seem to fit, or an identity doesn't seem to align with one of your wants – don't worry! As you learn more about the Mindset, Habits, and Words related to your *Magnetic Faith*, you'll understand not only how to think about these wants correctly, but also how to bring them to life in a God-glorifying manner.

You are unique, an heir, new, free, destined, loved, and powerful. The life you are meant to be living is closer than you think. The God who created you is ready for you to accept and walk in these truths. Your journey towards a truly *Magnetic Faith* has just begun.

Part 2: Magnetic Mindset

How To Transform Your Life By Renewing Your Mind

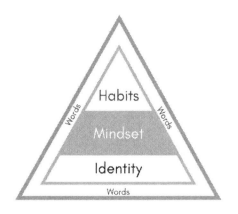

What Do We Mean When We Say "Mindset"?

At the end of 2017, I began to get very sick. I was nauseous all of the time, there was a sharp pain in my abdomen, and I felt incredibly weak. As the days turned into weeks, I slept less and less as the pain grew worse. Everything I ate hurt my insides, so I ate less and less until I was only eating a cup of soup a day. My body became a shadow of its former self. I lost 25% of my total body weight in under 3 months and honestly believed I might die.

Over this period, I saw thirteen different doctors. Thirteen! General practitioners, gastroenterologists, immunologists, oncologists... All of them ran their own set of tests, but none of them could tell me exactly what was happening to my body. Everyone agreed that something was wrong, but no one knew what it was or how to fix it. So I continued to be in pain, to wither, and to lose hope.

All of it came to a breaking point about 4 months later. I had been on short-term disability for months at this point, and my ability to stay on it (which meant being able to keep my job and pay our bills) was coming to an end. Either I would get better soon, or this spiral was about to get exponentially worse. I decided to take one more recommendation and try one last doctor who specialized in functional internal medicine.

She had a completely different approach. Instead of spending all of our time together trying to figure out what had gone wrong, she spent her energy trying to make me healthy again. Her different perspective gave me hope that whatever this was, wasn't going to last forever. There was something I could do, right now, that would begin to change my health for the better.

I'll never forget what she said in our first meeting together: "From this point forward, everything you put into your body, everything you do with your body, and every thought you think about your body is either going to move you closer to or further from health."

Your mindset works the same way.

Mindset is an established way of thinking, or as I like to think of it – a series of worn paths through your brain. When you see a face or smell a food or hear a song, your brain has to decide what to do with that stimulation. The easiest thing for it to do is to repeat what it has always done. If the face is of someone you love, your brain makes you smile. If the food is one of your favorites, your brain increases your saliva. If the song is one you know by heart, your brain will lead you to begin singing along.

Your brain makes the choice for you based upon all of the previous choices it has witnessed you make. This is a profoundly powerful tool, but also an incredibly dangerous one. This structure is why it's so difficult for us to break bad habits, and so easy for us to fall back into them.

But I'm here to tell you you have a choice.

You have the power and ability to rewrite your thinking and transform your mindset. You can absolutely develop a mind that relishes in the things of God and, as a result, attracts the things God has for you. The mind is a battlefield, a garden, and a tool and over the next several short chapters I am going to teach you how to harness everything it can be, so that you can start controlling the things that control you.

Read this next part very carefully: *From this point forward, everything you put into your mind, every thought you let it think, every voice you let it hear, every truth you tell it to believe is either going to move you closer to or further from the life you desire to live.*

It's been six months since the first meeting with that doctor and I am, quite literally, the healthiest I have ever been. Why? Because I took her advice seriously. I trusted that the healing transformation I needed required inner work before I would see outer results. I dedicated myself to conscious consumption, both physically and mentally. I saw the healthy body I wanted to create and I made the sacrifices to achieve it.

Once you accept the identities God has called you to walk in, nothing can hold you back. Nothing, that is, except for the limitations of your own thinking.

The 3 Dimensions of Your Mind

I believe everyone's mind fulfills 3 primary roles in their life: a tool, a battlefield, and a garden. All three have their own purposes, with some crossover. To not acknowledge one or more of these dimensions is to leave your mind, and therefore your life, open to unwanted destruction.

Your Mind is a Tool

First and foremost, your mind is a tool. It controls your body, how you walk, speak, and eat. It enables you to react to your environment: to jump out of the way of a distracted driver or to feel emotion during a live play. It also shapes our lives.

Your mind can be a rope you use to help you climb up to new levels of living. It can also be a hammer with which you smash possibility. Your mind can fix problems or worsen them. It can plug a leak in your soul or expand it.

What I want you to understand is that your mind is *capable*. Capable of feats beyond your imagination, but also of destruction beyond your greatest fears. However, its capability is limited by its user. I could be given the same toolbelt as a master craftsman and would have no idea how to use half the things in there! Even though I had the same tools as the craftsman, I wouldn't be able to produce the same results right away because my skill and training doesn't compare to his.

In the same way, I want to show you that your mind is capable of accomplishing anything – so long as you are willing to develop the skills needed to use it properly.

Your Mind is a Battlefield

Joyce Meyer's excellent book, *Battlefield of the Mind*, shot this idea into the public consciousness. She helped us see how our minds are in a constant war to believe and trust and pursue the things of God. The battle ensues because of the world around us, as well as the "world" we have allowed to take up root inside of us.

I love this analogy because war is not a light activity. It's not a hobby you take up or something you choose to do when it fits your schedule. War is aggressive. It interrupts your normal life and calls you to rise to the occasion. To win a war requires training, sacrifice, and strategy. War does not end because you are tired or when you have lost a single battle. It only ends when the enemy is defeated.

I want to make this very clear: your mind is NOT the enemy, only the area where the enemy comes to do battle. Your mind is beautiful, but it needs you to fight for it. It needs you to step up and train and sacrifice. Your life depends on it.

Your Mind is a Garden

The garden of your mind will produce the life you lead it to grow. My mother has a green thumb. When my office plant began to wither and die (because I may have forgotten to water it…for a few weeks), I brought it to her. Within a month, the plant was not only thriving once again, but it had grown so much she had to cut it in half and place part of it into another pot. My mother understands how to help plants flourish, and is able to accomplish amazing feats of creation because of this.

As I said above, everything you allow into your mind will either help it or hurt it. Like a garden, you get to determine what grows. You have the power to till the soil, choose the fruits and vegetables and flowers, and uproot the weeds. Your garden will grow whatever you tell it to, so long as you also do the work to make that growth possible.

A beautiful mind is the result of someone's labor. If you want possibility and Godly trust to be your defaults (rather than fear and lack), this is possible. If you see someone living a life similar to the one you feel called to live (as in running a business or nonprofit, full-time ministry, writing, painting, dancing, parenting, etc.) – you can be sure that the outward fruit of their life is a result of the inner garden they have tended to for years.

Because you are a child of God, your "soil" is ready to produce extraordinary things. Now you just need the tools to do so.

These three analogies have helped me tremendously on my faith journey. They have helped me see how my identity connects to everything else in my life. The mind is the connection. It is the delivery system for truth when used correctly, and the source of pollution when misused. Once you accept yourself to be unique, an heir, new, free, destined, loved, and powerful – it becomes the mind's duty to play these out.

For example, believing that you are new can be a tool to drive life transformation. But to truly have this new belief take root requires that you work hard at it (as in tilling the soil) – by presenting yourself with evidence (as we saw in *Magnetic Identity*), fighting the counterproductive thoughts that enter your mind (this is the battlefield part), and integrating the additional lessons we will learn in the coming parts.

For now, I want you to have these three positions in the back of your mind as we continue moving forward. Every lesson in this part will help you master one of those three areas: develop your ability to use the mind as a tool, equip you to win the battle in your mind, and give you the skills needed to make the garden flourish.

A Note on the Accuser

When he [the devil] lies, he speaks his native language, for he is a liar and the father of lies. John 8:44b

I have to warn you, the journey to renewing your mind and adopting a magnetic mindset will not be an easy one. It will not happen overnight. There will be days where the struggle feels like it is too much, like the challenge too big. I want to tell you that is a lie.

On your journey towards magnetism – by which I mean confidence, faith, expectation, hope, strength, and abundance – you will encounter an enemy. That enemy is Satan. Satan, or the devil, is many things, but when it comes to your thought life there is one title which captures his manipulative strategy: *accuser*.

The devil cannot make you *do* anything. He is like a dog on a leash. God allows him to go only so far and no further. He is allowed to bark only so loud and that's it. Everything about him is limited by God's grace and power and so ultimately, we are safe.

When it comes to our minds, the devil's strongest attack is his ability to feed us lies, or more accurately, accusations. He tries to convince us that what we did was unforgivable – that who we are is dirty and undeserving and unworthy of love. All of his energy is spent trying to achieve a single goal: doubt.

Doubt is his goal because he knows that is how he shuts off the magnet. If we begin to doubt who God says we are and what He promised us, then we are engaging in the opposite of faith. We are exchanging confidence and expectation for fear and distrust. Doubt weakens our resolve and saps our energy. It makes us question the most fundamental truths about who we are and allows Satan to establish "a foothold" – a way for him to make the accusations even louder.

In Matthew 4:1-11, we see Jesus being tempted in the desert. This had to be the most difficult thing Jesus endured up to that point in his life. So what strategy did the devil use? He tried to make Jesus doubt his identity with accusations: *"IF you are the Son of God..."* then you would be able to do this, or you would already have that. Satan knew that the strongest weapon in his arsenal was the ability to cast doubt through accusation, and that is what he brought against Jesus – God himself in the flesh.

But it didn't work! We see Jesus overcome the accuser three times. And all three times Jesus fought back with the same weapon: the Word of God.

Just as in the identity work, where we used Biblical evidence to help us understand who we really are – when it comes to renewing our minds, our strongest asset will be our knowledge of God's Word. The Bible is

THE tool we must use to confirm our identity and secure our mind. This is what Jesus used and this is what we must use as well.

In the coming parts, we will learn how to go on the offensive with our magnetic faith. But before we can achieve those goals, there are some principles we must first master.

Believe Before You Think

"What are you waiting for? You're faster than this. Don't think you are, know you are." - Morpheus

In the movie The Matrix (*which is tied for my favorite movie of all time*), Morpheus and Neo prepare to have their first battle within a simulated dojo. Neo has just spent hours downloading every type of martial arts known to man into his brain. Because of what he knows, he should be a master. He should be unbeatable.

The fight begins and Morpheus clearly has the upper hand. He anticipates every one of Neo's moves, dodging and striking as if the whole exercise is a bore. Neo tries harder and harder, but you can see the frustration wearing on him. Finally, Morpheus kicks him into a wooden beam and sends Neo flying to the ground.

"Why was I able to beat you?" Morpheus asks. Neo replies that he is faster, stronger, and better trained. Morpheus challenges him – in this place, none of that matters. Because it's a simulation, they are basically equals. The only difference being what they believe is possible. Morpheus then tells him to stand and challenges his belief with the above quote: "What are you waiting for? You're faster than this."

Something clicks in Neo's mind. He believes it. He believes that the only limitations he has are the ones he placed upon himself. So he begins fighting back harder and faster than before. The onlookers are stunned, they've never seen anyone move that fast before. Within seconds of this mind shift, Neo pins Morpheus against the wall and wins the round.

I love this scene because it demonstrates so perfectly the difference between knowledge and belief. Neo had all the knowledge he needed in order to win the battle, but he lacked belief. Without belief, knowledge is powerless to attain the victories we desire. In order to achieve what we want, we must have both.

Most Christians spend their time building their knowledge, which, don't get me wrong, is excellent! We listen to sermons, read great books, and engage in group Bible studies. Yet, we often see little change for all our efforts. We stay stuck in habitual sins, destructive relationships, and continually fall short of the version of ourselves we know we could become.

This is why understanding the difference between belief and knowledge is so essential. Knowledge is the tool which can achieve the desired result. Belief is how we activate the tool. Knowledge is the kind of plants we want to see grow in our garden. Belief is the soil which makes growth possible.

In the next part, you will learn what beliefs must be in place before you can take full advantage of the knowledge you already have. These beliefs will make the activation of your faith and the transformation of your life not only possible but inevitable.

The 7 Magnetic Beliefs

Over the next several pages you will discover seven of the most fundamental and powerful mindsets I have come across over my years of study, growth, challenge, and ultimately success.

I guarantee some, if not all, of these will challenge many of your deeply held beliefs. Good! Your beliefs are what have crafted the life you currently live. So if you want something different, if you desire a different reality, then digging up and replacing old, ill-fitting beliefs is the correct next step.

Our minds are complex in their construction, but simple in their operation. There are clear steps you can take to create the kind of mind you want. And those are exactly what I will show you in the pages that follow.

Mindset 1: Growth Over Fixed

"We like to think of our champions and idols as superheroes who were born different from us. We don't like to think of them as relatively ordinary people who [became] extraordinary." — Carol Dweck

In 1884, when the engineers were putting the finishing touches upon the Washington Monument, they wanted to adorn the top of it with a precious metal. They wanted a shiny, gleaming spectacle. Something people would know was valuable and would stand the test of time. The team didn't have an unlimited budget, but they had enough to make this aspect of the build really stand out. So they chose one of the most in-demand precious metals at the time: aluminum.

Aluminum's value sat right in between gold and silver in that day. Depending on who you ask, the aluminum pyramid they created to sit atop the monument was valued up to $300,000 in today's dollars.[iii] It was everything they wanted and they thought it would always be that way. Until something changed.

In the late 1880s, less than a decade later, scientists and entrepreneurs found a way to extract aluminum more easily, therefore creating much more of it and driving its value down. Today, that same amount of aluminum which was once as valuable as a brand new home is barely worth $500.

Why am I sharing this story? Because I want to illustrate the point that things you believe may be written in stone, unchangeable, and "fixed" may, in reality, be on the very cusp of dramatic transformation.

In her book, *Mindset*, author and researcher Carol Dweck illustrates the difference between two mindsets. The first, which she calls a "fixed" mindset, represents the vast majority of people. They believe things are the way they are and that's the way they will always be. Their surroundings and circumstances dictate what is possible. They learn to accept life as it is and do little to push against it, because at their deepest core – they don't believe change is possible.

The second mindset, and the belief I will urge you to adopt, is called the "growth" mindset. This belief is defined by possibility. A growth-minded person understands that everything is malleable. The world as we know it is the product of both the people who came before us and the people who are around now. And since we are here, we have an opportunity to make real change. Most importantly, we can change. We can improve, transform, bloom, and flourish. Our circumstances and surroundings are not the end-all be-all of our existence. Change is possible.

Like the aluminum example, there are some things in our lives which seem unchangeable. We live over 100 years after this dramatic shift occurred. We line our grills with aluminum foil bought for a dollar and don't think twice about tossing it out afterward. Could you imagine doing that with gold? It sounds ridiculous! But then again, so do some of the things you may want to change in your own life.

What things seem impossible or insurmountable? Maybe it's an addiction you've carried for over 15 years or a job you want to leave but are scared you wouldn't be able to care for your family without. Maybe it's a health issue that has defined and limited your existence as long as you can remember. Whatever it is, it will limit your ability to hold a magnetic mindset until you adopt this belief. The belief of growth, that change is possible, that fixed things can be transformed.

You don't have to convince yourself, yet, that change *will* happen or that transformation is around the corner. I've found those ideas to be overwhelming at times and even discouraging when they don't seem to be happening. Instead, all I am asking is that you question your assumptions. You doubt what was once undoubtable.

You invite God to do the impossible simply by acknowledging the impossible is an option.

Mindset 2: Results Over Failure

"Success is stumbling from failure to failure with no loss of enthusiasm." — Winston S. Churchill

Chances are you have heard the story of Thomas Edison experimenting with literally thousands of different combinations before he found one that made his lightbulb work. Maybe you've also heard of Harland Sanders, the founder of KFC, and how it took approximately 1009 restaurant owners saying "no" to his chicken recipe before he received his first "yes."

We hear these stories and are amazed because of how often a single "no" has completely stopped us in our tracks. When I was growing up, I was a rule-follower. The scariest thing in the world to me was getting into trouble so I did everything I could possibly do to avoid it. I spent every brain cell and energy molecule being perfect because anything else meant something horrible would happen. Being imperfect meant I was a failure. Being a failure meant I was unlovable.

That mindset carried into my adulthood and impacted the way I handled setbacks. The first time I told my graduate advisor I wanted to be a professor like him, he told me "no, I don't think that is a good idea." Rather than trying to prove him wrong, and possibly fail, I decided to seriously reevaluate my path and see what my options were. I let his "no" define me.

When I started my very first business where I managed the social media accounts for local businesses, I got my first few customers through cold calling (probably the most difficult thing I had ever done up to that point in my life). To this day I still remember the noes I received. After a few dozen noes, I went back to the drawing board and tried a different business. And then another one after that.

If I look back at my life, as painful as it might be to admit, my path has been shaped more often by the noes and fear, then by yeses and courage. But the good news, for me and for you, is that we have the ability to choose differently.

Tony Robbins writes, "There is no such thing as failure. There are only results." What if, like Thomas Edison, we started to see every wrong path as an opportunity to learn and do better – rather than a shame-filled, life-altering moment? What if we treated our lives like experiments, allowing room for error and re-dos because nothing great was ever accomplished the first go-around? What if we gave our selves the grace to be told no, and then had the courage to tell ourselves yes anyways?

In order for God to accomplish everything He has for you and in you, you have to learn to be okay with the process. In my book, Crowned with David, I discovered that what made David the most successful king in Israel's history was not his wisdom or wealth or bravery. Instead, it was his ability to rise again after failure.

"David's extraordinary reign as king was a direct byproduct of his willingness to continually seek forgiveness and walk in that forgiveness. He is the model for how to succeed God's way... The people of God do not succeed by always doing things the right way - that is impossible. The people of God succeed by consistently taking bold action and when they fail, they don't give up. They turn to God, ask for forgiveness, and continue to pursue God and their calling as they walk in their forgiveness."[iv]

You have something extraordinary to add to this world. But the only way it will come to pass is if you accept that your attempts to bring it to life will be marked by bumps and bruises, shame and insecurity, failure and forgiveness. All I ask is that you don't stop trying.

Mindset 3: Abundance Over Scarcity

"When you realize there is nothing lacking, the whole world belongs to you." – Lao Tzu

I want you to put yourself in the shoes of one of Jesus' disciples for a minute. Imagine that days of healing and miracle-working have culminated in an audience of thousands listening to Jesus teach. As the afternoon turns into evening, you notice the fatigue on the people's faces. They're excited, thankful – but also tired and very hungry. You know they're going to have at least an hour walk back to their towns so you ask Jesus to wrap it up.

Jesus looks back at you with a strange look. Not anger, maybe surprise. *Why* He asks?

They're hungry and it's getting late, you reply.

You give them something to eat.

Your stomach drops. Something inside you almost knew Jesus was going to say something like that. How in the world am I supposed to give them something to eat? All I see is this lunch, some bread...a fish. It's barely enough for me and Jesus let alone a crowd!

Jesus sees your frustration and motions for you to bring what you have over. You hand him the small basket and He begins to tear the food apart. He gives you a handful to deliver to the small family sitting over there. So you do. You give them the food and on your way back you notice Jesus is still tearing the food apart. But how? In fact, he's sending all the disciples off with handfuls to deliver but the food doesn't seem to be running out. Actually, it seems like every time a disciple returns the pile is actually bigger than when they left.

Kris Vallotton writes "It was in the nature of Jesus to behave extravagantly." I think this story illustrates Kris's statement perfectly. Whenever Jesus provides for others in the Bible, He does so extravagantly. Whether it's wine or food or money – Jesus never gives *just enough*. The baskets are always overflowing. The pitchers are constantly running over.

These are just a microcosmic scale of the abundance God wants us to experience. Did you know that the sun dumps more energy on earth in a single hour than the entire human population uses in a year? Or that if all plants stopped producing oxygen tomorrow, the earth could still sustain 7 billion people for 50 million more years?[v]

God has quite literally built abundance into the fabric of His creation. He molded the world to be a reminder that in Him, there is always more than enough. But in order to access it, we must believe.

The scarcity mindset is the opposite. It believes that there is never enough. That lack is the rule, not the exception. And we find evidence for this belief everywhere. Growing up I saw my parents struggle. Then, when they got divorced I saw them struggle even more. I learned to pray prayers not from a place of confident provision, but from fearful desperation.

Like the disciples, I believed that all I could see was all there was. But with Jesus, that's never the case. Abundance may be hiding, but it is never gone. Where Jesus is, scarcity cannot be. It's like the light being turned on in a dark room. The darkness has to flee.

The same applies to believing in and for God's abundance. When this belief begins to take root, scarcity has to flee. Is has to shrivel up and make room for God's intended order. Then you will start to see abundance not as the exception, but the rule. You'll begin to understand that God's miracles were not for some other person in some other time and now they've run out.

Nothing God gives ever runs out. Nothing God does ever comes up short. He always gives, does and is more. Abundance is in His nature. As you shift your mindset, you'll realize it's in yours as well.

Mindset 4: Tortoise Over Hare

"The Lord is not slow in keeping his promises, as some understand slowness." 2 Peter 3:9a

One of my favorite Dave Ramsey stories is from the time he got to sit down with a billionaire and pick his brain on business advice. As you could imagine, Dave was pretty excited. Here was this titan of industry whose knowledge and wisdom were being laid open for Dave's consumption. After a few minutes of small talk, Dave Ramsey asked him what the most important thing he could do to replicate the billionaire's success was. The man looked him straight in the eye and said it's all laid out in a single book.

What book you ask... *The Tortoise and the Hare.*

I know what you're probably thinking. *That's a children's book and I already know what it's about.* Yes, it is a children's book and yes, you probably do know the moral of the story. That slow, steady, directed steps will always beat rushed, directionless bursts. Even if the bursts are more fun. Even if everyone is encouraging you to rush because that's what they're doing.

But the tortoise mindset is also about so much more.

In the Bible, things almost never move as quickly as we would like them to. God promises Abraham an heir, but then made him wait decades until Isaac was born. Job cried out to God for any kind of answer, but had to endure weeks of physical, emotional, and mental anguish before it came. Jesus came to earth to plant the seeds of His kingdom, but first lived 30 years as an unknown carpenter.

Time in the Bible seems to be a luxury. Promises appear to take forever, and God looks as though He enjoys watching us wait. But there is more at work beneath the surface.

When done correctly, moving slowly is an act of power. God does not have to rush because He already knows the end from the beginning. He has answered the "what ifs" and prepared for every twist and turn. He moves at His own pace because no one has the power to slow him down. For God, time is never a hindrance, only another tool within His tool belt. It's entirely at His disposable, ready to be molded to His will. Oftentimes, the more time there is to work with – the more beautiful the end result can be.

We are invited into this same power. When we acknowledge who we are in God, time stops being our enemy and becomes our tool. When the Bible calls us to "cease striving" (Psalm 46:10), it's calling us to quit being the hare. We must shift our thinking from "I must make this happen" to "Because of God, it is already done."

This belief will forever change the way we move. When done correctly, a slow-moving Christian moves from a place of confidence and purpose. Fearful Christians tend to move quickly. They rush around, fearing that if they stop they will fail and everyone will see how imperfect they are. Slow movers aren't afraid to let their scars be seen because their worth is never up for debate.

So what am I asking you to believe with this mindset? More than patience, more than consistency, more than anything – I want you to understand that you have the power to move at whatever pace God calls you to because He is the one who will make your path straight. And no matter how much faster you think you might be able to get "there" on your own, the shortest distance between two points will always be a straight line – and that is what God offers. Keep your eyes on Him, and He will make sure you cross that finish line.

Mindset 5: Focus Over Fad

"The man who chases two rabbits catches neither." –
Confucius

During 2017, I spent over 6 months consuming everything I could on the subject of purpose. I read books, listened to sermons, and watched Ted talks all in the effort to understand this concept better. My research led me to write *What The Bible Says About Purpose*. In this book, I lay out the foundational, Biblical principles you need to follow in order to both discover and fulfill your purpose. The piece I want to share with you right now is one of my favorite lessons from that book: the purpose killer.

Most people assume fear is the purpose killer and for good reason. Fear can be debilitating. It can rob us of our ambition if we let it. But even with how destructive fear may be, there is a more deceptive entity at work wrecking our purpose journeys – and in turn, switching off our ability to develop a magnetic faith. This enemy is distraction.

Distraction is an interruption of our attention. The origin of the word means to literally be pulled apart. Purpose is a result of fostering a magnetic mindset. Therefore, whatever attacks it also attacks our ability to be, think, do and have all that God intends for us.

The good news is distraction can be defeated. It can be overcome with two simple steps:

- Step 1: Identify what distracts us.
- Step 2: Re-engage our focus on the right thing.

I call the things that distract us *fads*. The word distraction carries with it a negative connotation, so when I tell you to identify the distractions in your life – your first reaction will be to look for the destructive habits or sinful pleasures you know pull you away from what you should be doing and thinking. But that's not all that distracts us. More often we are distracted by good things, exciting things, and even beneficial things.

We don't call church volunteering opportunities or work promotions or an impromptu weekend with friends a distraction because we don't see them as bad things. And they're not, in and of themselves, bad. What makes them a distraction or a fad (something quick, exciting, but ultimately unhelpful) is how they pull you away from what's important.

So this is where step two comes in: we must refocus upon what matters. The fact is, whatever we focus on will grow. But in order for growth to occur, we have to aggressively protect ourselves from being pulled apart. This will only happen when focus transitions from something we think we should do, to something we believe is essential to creating the life we, and God, desire us to live.

Focus requires us to be brave. It requires us to believe that what we have in front of us is the right thing. That the direction we're moving in is correct. And that the God we are trusting is faithful.

Distractions offer us a false sense of safety because they provide us with scapegoats. I've never met a distraction that didn't eventually become an excuse. Focus gives us nothing to fall back on or hide behind. It leaves us out in the open, exposed and vulnerable. And yet, while being out in the open may attract unwanted challenges – it's also the only way to attract God's blessings.

Focus is not for the faint of heart because its rewards are much too bountiful for them to carry. But you, reading this, are not faint. And in this moment, you are not distracted. You are on the right path, moving in the right direction, opening yourself up so that focus can begin to transform your life.

Mindset 6: Authenticity Over Acceptance

"You are the only you there is and ever will be. I repeat, you are the only you there is and ever will be. Do not deny the world its one and only chance to bask in your brilliance." – Jen Sincero

Ask any food aficionado and they will tell you there is a HUGE difference between authentic international food and Americanized versions of the same dishes. Taco Bell and Chipotle are nothing like true Mexican cuisine, and nothing on their menus even remotely resembles a true Puerto Rican dish. Olive Garden does not truly deliver an Italian experience, nor do mall Chinese restaurants offer the richness of genuine Asian food.

These restaurants serve a purpose and have found some measure of success because they valued acceptance over authenticity. They were created to reach and satisfy as many people as possible so that they could earn as large a profit as possible. In doing so, compromises had to be made. The flavors were subdued so that they could reach a wider audience. The sweetness was increased to fit with an American palate. Small, incremental changes stacked up until the creators had a product people enjoyed, but that had lost touch with its original inspiration.

These accepted foods may taste fine, but they will never be everything they were meant to. They will never earn a Michelin star (the highest award in the culinary field). They won't cause people to cherish the meal or tell stories about their experience. The food, while satisfying, will ultimately be forgettable. The restaurants will make money until palates change. And no true change will occur because of their existence.

You face these same options.

On the one hand, you can choose to adopt the belief that acceptance is the best way forward. This path will have fewer challenges and roadblocks because it has been traveled millions of times before. The road is well-worn and you'll find plenty of signage explaining how to move along it. There will be simple, satisfying rewards and you will probably come out the other end having lived a fine life. People will like you, things won't always be easy – but certainly not that hard, and while compromises seemed to have defined your existence, they became easier to make as time went on. This is option one.

Option two is much more difficult. Option two requires you to take a stand. To believe that you are not a mistake. You are not here for your flavors to be subdued or to become unnecessarily sweet. You are violently original, and because of that, not everyone will accept you. In fact, at times it will appear that most people are actually opposed to you. You frighten them because you are a glowing reminder of what they are not: original. Being authentic means you are willing to trade the small rewards of certainty and comfort for the immense gifts of adventure and transformation.

Option two is the only way to have an impact upon the world. Authenticity is the only way to exhibit a magnetic faith. God cannot give you what is uniquely yours if you spend your energy denying who you truly are.

> "If you belong to the world, it would love you as its own." John 15:19

I am not here to tell you that there are not real, satisfying rewards for choosing a life of acceptance. That would be a lie. Rather, I am here to tell you that the rewards for being authentic are better. A commitment to authenticity is the prerequisite for the extraordinary.

Mindset 7: God Is For You Not Against You

If God is for us, who can be against us? He who did not spare his own Son, but gave him up for us all—how will he not also, along with him, graciously give us all things?
Romans 8:31b-32

The final belief I want to share with you is the basis for everything we have talked about up to this point in the *Magnetic Mindset* portion. Everything rests on this belief being firmly grounded in your conscious and unconscious thoughts. It is the foundation upon which everything else stands. If you can get this belief to truly take hold in your soul of souls, you will be unstoppable.

God is for you.

I think in our Christian culture, we have stripped this phrase of its scandalous power and have tried to make it "reasonable." We might think, yes God is for us as long as we are involved in ministry – or praying unselfishly – or checking all the spiritual boxes. We place unnecessary constraints around this idea of God's support because the idea that it might be unrestrained is too much.

The concept that God might actually be for us, not as a means to an end, but purely for the sake that we are his children and He loves us and wants good things for us is too much to handle. But what if it's true?

What if the most unrestrained, undeserved, unlimited version of this was the truth? That God is all in for who you are and what you want. That the God of all grace and all power is not up there waiting for you to get everything in order before He can overwhelmingly bless your life. Rather, He's already beside you, cheering you on, asking you to ask Him, pushing you to trust Him, steering your affections towards grander things – not so that you can be disappointed and settle "for what God has." But so that you can be stirred to want beyond what you thought was possible, and then, as you realize how true this belief really is, aim to have ambition "for what God has."

God being for you requires you to be for yourself. If we look back again to the example of Jesus in Matthew 4, we see Jesus do a few important things. First, He jealously guards His space and time both before and after the temptation. Jesus understood that self-care is the foundation for other-care, and He could only give peace, health, hope and so much more if He first prioritized those things for Himself. Second, He was able to deny the devil's offers because He believed in the *better* God had for Him. Jesus chose to activate His knowledge of God through belief, and therefore secure the power He needed to overcome.

Like Jesus, we always have a choice. We can choose to activate our power through belief or forfeit by acting on our fears. We can believe things about God which make us afraid to ask and risk, or we can believe in a Heavenly Father who is in our corner. One who joyfully challenges us to live a life beyond what is humanly possible. One of possibility, of expectation, and of faith.

God being for you is simultaneously the greatest treasure and the greatest responsibility you could ever encounter. It requires you to actively seek out the better God has for you and to champion it in your mind above all else. Above distracting temptations, above false beliefs and fads, above small desires.

God is for you in the most ambitious sense of the phrase. It's up to you to activate this benefit through belief, and this is where the magnetic mindset comes into play.

Framing

We began learning how to create a *Magnetic Mindset* by discussing the dimensions of our minds. How our mind can act as a tool, a garden, and a battlefield – and how understanding the differences between these can help us achieve our goals. From there we touched on the danger of doubt and the difference between belief and knowledge. This led us to examining seven magnetic beliefs which can activate both the knowledge we have and the identities which are lying dormant within us.

As we close this section of the *Magnetic Faith* structure, I want to bring all of the above ideas together into a single concept. In psychology, researchers have found that there are dozens of ways to influence the decisions a person will make. These can be used for good outcomes (convincing someone to make healthier life choices) or not so good ones (driving people to spend money on unnecessary purchases). These techniques can be powerful persuasion tools because most of the time, no one knows they are being used. They simply blend in with the conversation or product and subversively influence the outcome without the subject knowing.

However, once a person is made aware of these – the power flips. Suddenly, they are the ones in control because they are now aware of the "invisible" influences which were directing their decisions, and therefore, their actions. One of the most powerful of these techniques is called the Framing Effect.

The Framing Effect is "when people make different choices based on how a decision/problem is presented or interpreted."[vi] Now, if you have ever been asked if the glass is half-empty or half-full, you have already encountered this principle. Another example would be you telling someone they have a 25% chance of winning or a 75% chance of losing. In the Framing Effect, the situational facts do not change. The cup is at half point either way; the percentages tell the same story. Rather, what changes is the presentation of the situation.

This is where all the power lies because how you describe a situation to yourself or others ALWAYS influences the choices and actions that follow. People buy more when there are sale signs posted, whether or not the actual prices have changed. People take more risks when the upsides are talked about more often than the downsides. And your faith, when described in the proper ways, can be used to transform your life.

Everything in this *Magnetic Mindset* book was written to help you frame your situations differently. Your God-given identity is the foundation for ambitious thinking. And ambitious, magnetic, God-centered thinking is less about changing *what* you think and more about changing *how* you think.

In this life, and as the best version of yourself, you are still going to have to face thoughts about paying a huge bill, taking a big risk, or standing up for your true self. These thoughts will want to bring with them feelings of fear, anxiety, and overwhelm. If I tried to tell you that you would never have to deal with these kinds of things if you truly develop a magnetic faith that would be dishonest and unhelpful. A better strategy is to be honest about the challenges you will face and equip you to face those challenges in a completely different fashion. One in which gives you the upper hand in every trial and allows you to flourish as God intended.

The seven magnetic beliefs I've given you are the frames with which I want you to describe every situation you encounter. In everything, I want you to believe that you have…

- the capability to grow,
- access to abundance,
- the ability to produce results,
- the confidence to move slowly,
- the discipline to focus,
- the courage to be authentic,
- the assurance that God is on your side.

Your brain is beautiful. Your mind is a gift. With it, you can quite literally remake your world.

As you use these frames to think magnetically, you will invite the blessing of God to transform your life. But be prepared, because the mind needs an outlet. Our thoughts, if they are going to accomplish what we desire, need to be set loose into the world. And their vehicle of choice is action.

"The mind is the leader or forerunner of all actions." – Joyce Meyer

Now we must learn the next step on our journeys toward a truly *Magnetic Faith*. How to drive our *Magnetic Mindset* into actions that can change the world. Get ready to encounter *Magnetic Habits*!

How To Create And Control Your Mindset

If you're ready to hit the ground running and begin reshaping your mind, I've included a few practical steps to follow below. Although your mindset is just one piece of the *Magnetic Faith* triangle, it can be the most difficult piece to master. I pray these guidelines help you do just that.

1. **Continue Reading.** Yes, I said it again! If you review the *triangle of what controls you* once more, you'll see that the mindset sits right in the middle of everything: above the identity, below the habits, and within the words. This structure is purposeful. Even though I am about to give you a few mindset-specific tools, I want you to understand the most effective way to reshape your mindset is to continue on the journey towards understanding how the entire triangle works together. Your identity and habits have as great an effect upon your mind as it does on them. So if you want true transformation, it must

come from all angles – or all pieces of the triangle – if it is going to truly last.

2. **Feed The Right Wolf.** There's a Native American parable called *The Tale of Two Wolves* which goes like this:

A grandfather talks with his grandson and says there are two wolves inside each of us which are always at battle.
One is a good wolf which represents things like kindness, bravery, and love. The other is a bad wolf which represents things like greed, hatred, and fear.
The grandson stops and thinks about it for a second. Then he looks up at his grandfather and asks, "Grandfather, which one wins?" The grandfather replies, "The one you feed."[vii]

When it comes to the battle for your mind, the same principle applies. You are going to be continually inundated with beliefs – ideas that either "feed" your ability to believe in growth, abundance, results, confidence, focus, authenticity, and God-support; or thoughts that want to keep you stuck in fixed, failure, scarcity, rushing, fad, compromising, and helpless mindsets. The food comes in the form of what you listen to, what you watch, who you talk to, and how you spend your downtime. Every day your consumption will feed one of those two "wolves." Make sure you feed the one you want to win.

3. **Keep A Thought Journal.** One of the most beneficial mindset practices I've implemented in the last year was the creation of a thought journal. I was struggling with unhealthy thought patterns and my counselor helped me institute this practice in my daily life. It felt a little strange at first, but it wasn't long until I not only saw, but internally felt, the benefits of this exercise. Eventually, I could work the process in my mind without writing it down, although I still do at times because the added step of scribing has loads of other brain-activating benefits.

Here's how it works. Find a small journal or notepad you can carry around in your pocket during the day. When you feel yourself having an emotional reaction to something (like stress, worry, fear), pull out the journal and start this process.

I. Describe the situation (*i.e. I just got a bill I wasn't expecting*)
II. Identify what you feel (*fear, worry, etc.*)
III. Explain what thoughts automatically started coming to your mind (*things like this always happen to me, I can never catch a break*)
IV. Identify which of the 7 negative belief systems these thoughts fit under (*fixed,*

failure, scarcity, hare, fad, acceptance, no support)

V. Now, identify which of the 7 Magnetic Mindset belief systems you would like to frame this situation with *(growth, abundance, results, confidence, focus, authenticity, God-support)*

VI. Explain how the situation could turn out with the new positive mindset in place *(God will provide extravagantly, this is an opportunity for my faith to grow)*

VII. Identify the new feelings you have and want to have *(hope, confidence, etc.)*

The trick is to do this consistently. Every time your brain wants to run down old, familiar paths of scarcity, fear, and failure stop it in its tracks and direct it towards the thought-patterns you want it to think. This is the mental construction I mentioned earlier. This is the hard work which will transform your life from the inside out.

4. **Clean Your Room.** Over the past decade, lots of research has been done on the connection between people's environments and their mental health. The link is clear: people who cultivate environments which are clean and organized experience less stress, more clarity, and overall better mental health. It turns out when our parents yelled at us to clean our rooms, they really did have our best in mind! This step will look differently depending on your particular situation. My advice is to start small.

Find a small box and fill it with things you can donate (i.e. begin decluttering). If you're in a house or an apartment, take a Saturday afternoon and organize one-half of one room. Set the bar low. You don't want to have the thing that is supposed to help your mental garden flourish be the cause of its decline. The goal is to create a place that feeds the good "wolf" inside, so you'll have to figure out just what that looks like for you.

You are on your way to activating the growth, abundance, results, confidence, focus, authenticity, and God-support you were meant to live in. Already, your faith is becoming something truly magnetic. Keep going my friend. Your God-given destiny awaits.

Part 3: Magnetic Habits

How To Build The Actions That Will Get You To Where You Want To Be

What It Means To Have Faith

To wish was to hope, and to hope was to expect.
– Jane Austen

Positive expectations are the mark of the superior personality. – Brian Tracy

I've been in the habit of reading roughly a book a week for the last 6 years. During that time, I've had the opportunity to dive into the minds of literally hundreds of experts in the fields of science, history, theology, psychology, business, and more. I noticed pretty quickly that everyone had their own formula for success. Some preached immense focus and dedication; others opted for a more balanced approach. Some argued that we must take the long view in life; while still others were adamant about treating each day like it was your last.

The back and forth, while interesting, was also incredibly unhelpful. We go to books (non-fiction ones at least) for answers and direction – hoping that whatever we find in their pages might leap out and bring us closer to the life we are striving to build for ourselves.

Of all the pieces of advice I came across, there was one which consistently stuck in my mind as problematic. One idea which seemed almost universally accepted, yet it couldn't hold up against what I was seeing and understanding as the truth of Scripture. This idea can be boiled down to one question: what should we do with our expectations?

Most experts said we should either lower our expectations, so we wouldn't be disappointed, or give them up completely, so we could allow ourselves to be open to whatever life has for us. I want you to know that this isn't completely wrong, but it is definitely incomplete. Furthermore, this is the "worldly" way of dealing with life. If we did not have Jesus or the Bible, then I think these options would be perfectly legitimate ways of making our lives better and more joyful.

But here's the thing – we do have Jesus! We have a Word from God full of counterintuitive wisdom. Information that not only describes how things came to be but details how to continue the formation of God's Kingdom upon the earth. And with that - how to walk in power, abundance, and faith.

Now, this is faith...

> *"Faith is the assurance (deed, confirmation) of things hoped for (divinely guaranteed), and the evidence of things not seen [the conviction of their reality – faith*

comprehends as fact what cannot be experienced by the physical senses]." Hebrews 11:1 (AMP)

Before we move any further, let's also take a look at the definition and history of the word expectation. Expectation traces its roots back to Latin words meaning to "await" and "look out for." If we go one level deeper, we see the root word "expect" means to "regard as about to happen."[viii]

I hope you're starting to see the connection here. Both the verse in Hebrews and the definition point to the same conclusion: faith IS expectation.

To have faith is to wait on God, to actively look for His intervention, and to regard His work as about to happen. To be a Christian requires us to have faith. To have faith requires us to have expectations.

Abandoning all of your expectations is never an option for the Christian who is choosing to live by faith. When done properly, expectations can be transformed from an opportunity for disappointment to an avenue of God's divine intervention. Like everything in the Christian life, your expectations will have to be transformed, but they should not be tossed aside. They have far too important a role to play in your development.

Why Faith Is Dead Without Works

"The mind is the leader or forerunner of all actions." – Joyce Meyer

In James chapter 2, we find the author hammering away at what he deems a serious problem in the early church. These Christians aren't acting any differently than they did before they were saved. They're still showing favoritism, still letting their mouths run wild, and claiming to be faith-filled the entire time.

I could almost picture James pulling his hair while penning the letter. *How can you say that you have faith and yet show no difference in your life! This doesn't make any sense – someone please explain to me what these people are thinking!* I believe it's out of this frustration, and a deep regard for the true Gospel, that James pens the line he is most known for:

"In the same way, faith by itself, if it is not accompanied by action, is dead." James 2:17

Or put another way:

"So too, faith, if it does not have works [to back it up], is by itself dead [inoperative and ineffective]." James 2:17 (AMP)

Now it is one thing to talk about faith and works. This topic has been addressed by people much smarter than I, in books much bigger and more detailed than this one. Instead of readdressing the same idea, I want to approach it from a different angle. How do we think about expectations and actions?

By changing the wording just a little, a whole new world of examples open up to us. We go to work every day because we have the expectation that we will get a paycheck every two weeks. We go to the doctor when we are sick because we expect them to know how to make us healthy again. We exercise regularly (or at least we try) because we expect the work to benefit our bodies both now and in the long run.

Expectation always produces some sort of action.

If we expect to be promoted or rewarded, that expectation will drive us to work harder. If we expect to always lose or never catch a break, that expectation will drive us to give up or shut down. Every single action you take today from brushing your teeth to kissing your significant other good night is upheld by a framework of expectations. They are the fuel for what you do.

So then, if faith is expectation it must operate the same way. To have faith is to have your actions shaped by Godward expectation. A work-less faith is the product of an expectation-less life, and an expectation-less life is merely an empty existence.

You might be thinking: *I understand how faith and expectation are linked, and how actions relate – but is my faith really dead without actions?* Let me show you an example from nature to illustrate the point.

On our beautiful planet, most water sources are connected. Lakes become rivers which flow into oceans. Bodies of water dotted across our landscapes find avenues for reaching one another, constantly moving their contents through and around the world. This process keeps them alive.

However, there are a few bodies of water which through erosion and other natural shifts have become completely landlocked. These entities, known as endorheic basins or endorheic lakes, have a limited amount of water flowing in (mostly through rainfall and runoff), and no water flowing out.[ix] The water sits in these basins and lakes with no movement. The only way water can leave the lake is through evaporation. When the sun heats the water to a certain temperature, it becomes a gas and floats right on out of the stagnant pool. This process leaves behind all the salt and sediment which would normally be filtered by the process of a flowing stream. Over time, more water leaves, and more salt and sediment build up. This is how we get bodies of "water" like the Dead Sea – basins so full of salt, so thick with sediment, they become almost unrecognizable.

This is how your faith dies without works. If your faith is a pool of water being fed (flowed in) by good books, sermons, and Godly influences – it will grow. But in order for it to survive and thrive, it has to also flow out. If you are not engaging in regular actions, your faith will become stagnant. It will sit in its own pool of knowledge while the heat of life's frustrations and challenges begin to evaporate its life right before your eyes. Your faith will become salty and thick; condemning and prideful. And movement will become that much more difficult every day you choose to remain stuck.

Actions are the answer to keeping your faith alive. To making sure your expectations find the outflow they need for God to show up big in your circumstances.

The good news is that no matter how long your faith has been stagnant, it can be revived.

Transformed Expectations

What kinds of things should we expect as Christians? This is where the *triangle of what controls you* comes into play. Your expectations are fed from the bottom up. Your identity shapes your mindset. Your mindset shapes your habits. Your habits shape your words. And your words hold the entire structure together.

In the same way, what you expect is a byproduct of who you think you are and what you allow yourself to think. Expectation is a type of belief, so it makes sense that it must have a source. And you, reading this right now, can dictate what that source is, thereby controlling the expectations you want to experience.

A person who, at their core, sees themselves as unworthy of anything good (identity: unworthy, mindset: undeserving) will produce expectations that align with those beliefs. Then those expectations will guide what kinds of actions that person will or won't take. Example: *I'm not smart enough to do that job, therefore I won't apply for it.* So of course, the person does not get the job because they're identity and mindset *prevented them from taking steps towards making it a real option.*

The solution is to begin engaging the magnetic identities we spoke about in part 1. Exposing yourself to the truths of who you really are (unique, an heir, new, free, destined, loved, and powerful) is the only way to begin transforming your expectations.

I believe, wholeheartedly, that the Christian life is best lived when God's people fight fire with fire. Let me explain. We are often taught that in order to defeat sin or overcome bad habits, we have to really see them as terrible, horrible things. The belief is, once these things reach such a destructive nature in our minds we'll automatically start choosing the better, more helpful options. I can say from personal experience, this is just plain faulty thinking. It's never that simple. More than that, Jesus uses the exact opposite strategy when He ministered on earth.

Jesus did not recruit thousands of followers and infuriate the religious leadership by echoing how self-destructive the people were acting. Instead, He constantly, passionately communicated how much better His option was: the option to walk in the light, to turn away from sin, to invite God in. Jesus fought desire with desire. He transformed people not by showing them how dark their darkness was, but by emphasizing how bright their light could shine.

That's what I want for you. I want you to understand that the transforming of your expectations will only occur through the same strategy. Not through extreme self-denial, and shaming yourself over the destructive identities and mindsets you have carried. But your transformed expectations will come as you focus on who you really are: unique, an heir, new, free, destined, loved, and powerful. As you magnify these in your life, through exposing yourself to truth and following the guidance in the final parts of this series, you will learn how to fight fire with fire!

Then the cycle may continue, only now in a positive way. Instead of unhelpful identities and mindsets limiting your actions, helpful ones will inspire new actions (i.e. *Magnetic Habits*), because your expectations have been transformed by the renewal of your triangle.

Following the light will always lead you to better places than merely avoiding the dark.

Why Habits (And Not Just Actions) Are The Key

> We are what we repeatedly do. Excellence, then, is not an act, but a habit. – Aristotle

If you ask anyone who has been over our house for breakfast, they will all also tell you the same thing: I make great chocolate chip pancakes. Not to toot my own horn, but they are pretty great. I've worked hard over the years to get just the right batter consistency, the correct chocolate chip ratio, and the perfect timing on when to flip. When they're finished, the pancakes are a beautiful golden color and the guest gets a taste of chocolate in every single bite, but not too much. I'm proud of my pancakes, but they sure didn't start out that great.

My wife had the privilege of taste-testing the first few dozen batches as I improved the formula. Some pancakes were way too dry, while others remained goopy. Some were way too chocolatey (yes, it is possible), while you could be halfway through eating others without finding a single chocolate chip. They were a rollercoaster of outcomes, but over time – as I continued to cook and test and create – they started to take shape. The texture became more consistent. Then the chocolate chips became more even. Little by little, the pancakes became what they are today: excellent.

If I had given up after the first, second, or tenth time I made those pancakes, they would have never reached their full potential. It took time, patience, and repeated work to achieve the goal I had in mind. Part of the work was getting the right formula in place so that I would know *what* to do. The other part was developing the skills needed to apply the formula (aka *how* to do it).

Up to this point, you have been learning pieces of the formula which need to be in place: what identities are true about you and what mindsets you must adopt. In this part, we will begin to learn the *how*. It's important to realize that the activities covered in the pages to come are not one-off tests to see if God is watching. In order to get the full benefit of your Magnetic Faith, these actions must become habits.

Charles Duhigg, an author and researcher on the topic of habits, writes that nearly half of everything we do, we do out of habit and not from a place of conscious decision.[x] That means until you do the deep work of reforming your habits, you will always be working towards your goals with one hand tied behind your back. You might be immensely dedicated with the 50% you have control over, but if 50% continues to fall into old patterns – how much progress do you think you can really make?

What if I only worked on 50% of the pancake recipe? It would have never reached excellence. In the same way, the actions we will address must become habitual. They must ingrain themselves into your daily, weekly, monthly, and yearly patterns. That is the only way you will access their magnetic power.

Going to the gym for 8 hours in one day is much less beneficial than going to the gym for 30 minutes every other day for a month. Cooking 100 pancakes in a morning is less helpful than cooking 2 pancakes every Saturday for a year. Longevity, patience, routine, practice...habit. These are the words I want you to carry as we move into the next part of this book. These are the *how* that will transform your life.

Proclamation, Invitation and Evidence

Before we finally dive in and identity the 7 *Magnetic Habits* covered in this book, I felt led to call out two more ideas.

The first idea is this: expectations tend to be impatient. This is not necessarily a bad thing. But expectations can be fueled by high energy and high emotion, making them difficult to carry for long periods of time. That is why it's often easier to abandon expectations which seem unanswered. They can become spiritually and mentally exhausting. But if we look at the Bible, extended expectation is the breeding ground for God's greatest works.

Abraham's faith (expectation) carried his belief for a child for decades, until God finally answered that prayer through Isaac. Job's faith (expectation) for God to answer gave him the strength to refute his friends' bad theology until God himself spoke. Ruth's faith (expectation) that Naomi's God would provide supported her until Boaz could step up as God's means of provision.

Channeling your intense expectations into continued habits will develop your faith better than singular great acts of sacrifice or courage.[xi] God built this message into his creation. Trees that grow too fast during the summer are usually too thin to survive the winter. The stars that provide the most light are not the ones which burn themselves out, but the ones which steadily shine century into century.

God's timing seems slow until it doesn't. The lead up may seem long, but that's only because once He gets you going, there's no pausing on the fastlane of blessing.

The second idea comes from Isaiah and will help ensure we use the power of our *Magnetic Faith* correctly.

In Isaiah 10, the prophet proclaims how God will step in to undo the tyranny that has come by the hands of ungodly rulers. As we move through the text, Isaiah's prophecy grows more specific. From the unjust laws in the land to the specific oppression caused by Assyria, down to the current king sitting on Assyria's throne.

God has had enough of this ruler's pride. He rails against how bloated this man's ego has become. Then, in verse 15, Isaiah records two interesting sentences:

"Does the ax raise itself above the person who swings it, or the saw boast against the one who uses it? As if a rod were to wield the person who lifts it up, or a club brandish the one who is not wood!" Isaiah 10:15

The verse tells us this: no one can wield God.

God is not an ax we can swing around or a rod we can raise up whenever we like. God is not a tool we can use or an entity we can control. God is above and beyond us in every way we can imagine, and in a million ways we cannot.

I bring this up because the core message of *Magnetic Faith* is not that we can control God through what we think, do, and say. Instead, the core message is that by changing what we think, do, and say God can use us!

God is anxiously waiting (without the anxiety) for us to step into who and what we are so that He can shower us with who He is and what He has. Our magnetism is a means for God to move. Our identity shift is a proclamation that we are made to be used by God. Our mindset shift is an invitation to be used by God. And our habit shift is evidence that we are already being used by God – and ready for the more He has for us.

The 7 Magnetic Habits

As we move into the habits portion, I wanted to preface what you're about to read so that you can plan to get the most out of it. Of the 7 habits listed below: 3 you will be familiar with, 3 you may not be as familiar with, and the last 1 will require more explanation (which will lead us into the final part of *Magnetic Faith*).

For the ones you are familiar with, I want you to take your time to read through the short explanations as though these habits are brand new to you. Because if you don't, you will run the risk of ignoring the core habits which need to be in place in order for the rest of the entire *Magnetic Faith* triangle to work. These simple yet foundational habits are familiar for a reason: they're non-negotiable. They are evident in Scripture throughout the Old and New Testaments. They were as essential to Abraham's mission as they were to Jesus'. And if they mattered for them, then they must matter for us.

The second set of 3 consists of habits you may not be as familiar with. These are spiritual practices I've learned over the years from men and women who have dedicated their lives to following God and have ample fruit to show for it. Like the first 3, these habits are grounded in Scripture – but require more digging to discover. I've already done the "digging" work for you, so that you can focus on implementing these in your own life today.

The final habit will carry us into the last *Magnetic Faith* entry and allow us to fully integrate everything we have learned since page one. From my experience, this habit can be one of the most powerful avenues for change. But because of its power, it has also been the habit most responsible for keeping people stuck, depressed, and on the path to destruction. Power can go both ways, so I will show you how to exercise this habit correctly.

Habit 1: Take Your Bible Seriously

I have a friend who we'll call Peter. Now Peter is incredibly smart, a voracious reader, and one of the most creative people I know. He has overcome so much in his life, but there remains one area he hasn't ever been able to truly "win" at: his weight.

Peter is not overweight because he lacks knowledge – he's read more health and diet books than anyone I know. Peter is still overweight because of how he interacted with the knowledge he encountered. He would get a new book filled with helpful insights, take notes, tell me the cool things he learned – and then stop short of applying anything he just read.

Peter does not take the advice he receives seriously. How do I know that? Because none of his research has led him to productive, habit-shifting, life-changing action. He reads and learns and "grows", but ends up like the endorheic lakes we talked about above. All in-flow, no outflow.

So many of us do the same thing when it comes to God's Word. The first magnetic habit is not a call to read your Bible more but to read your Bible better. To treat it less like a textbook and more like a manual.

The last time I read a manual was when I put together a new coffee table my wife and I purchased from Ikea. The small white booklet had 37 steps. I didn't read it cover to cover before I began building the table. Instead, I read step 1 – gathered the necessary pieces – made the small connection it directed me to make – and then moved to step 2. It took time and I often had to read steps more than once to make sure I was following them correctly. But after about 40 minutes, I had a beautiful coffee table and a happy wife.

I WISH the Bible was as clear to follow as a manual, but that isn't the case. However, the *how* of reading a manual and taking your Bible seriously are very similar.

Read a step = Read a small portion of Scripture

Make sure you understand the pieces you need = Ask God for clarity and conviction on how you can apply His Word

Build the step = Take the action/apply the Scripture

Reading the Bible is active. It should push, poke, and prod your soul as you encounter it. Afterward, your actions should look different because of it. More than that, you should look different the next time you read Scripture because of the last time you read it.

The Bible is not an artwork you visit to observe. It is a whirlwind you get swept up in! This first magnetic habit is not to read your Bible more, but instead to read your Bible better: with vulnerability, passion, and above all with obedience. This is the kind of Scripture reading which will change your life.[xii]

Habit 2: Pray Like Your Life Depends On It

My best prayers have come out of times of distress. When I dropped out of college because I felt God calling me to ministry. When I had to go on short-term disability leave from work and the doctors had no idea how to help me. When I lost my job literally a month after getting married. These horrible, seemingly hopeless periods produced some of the most heart-wrenching, surrender-inducing prayers I've ever spoken in my life.

We see the same pattern in Scripture. Joshua sees that his army needs a miracle in order to win and so he cries out "Sun, stand still…" (Joshua 10:12). Elisha finds himself trapped with an unbelieving servant, surrounded by the Aramean army and prays "Strike the army with blindness" (2 Kings 6:18) Jabez was unwilling to stay in the painful circumstances of his upbringing and prayed "Bless me and enlarge my territory" (1 Chronicles 4:10).

When we feel that our backs are up against the wall, our prayers take on a whole new character. They become almost offensively bold. Who prays for God to stop the natural rhythm of the day? Who prays for thousands of men to become blind? Who prays to have so much supernatural favor, their painful beginning becomes a distant memory? People who have nothing to lose. People who know that without God's intervention, they'll be completely destroyed.

The good news is, you don't have to be in mortal danger in order to pray like this.

We normally see the pattern of prayer as operating in one direction. A comfortable life produces comfortable prayers while an extraordinary life leads to extraordinary prayers. However, prayer does not have to stay an "effect." It can become a cause. You can pray extraordinary prayers in the midst of a comfortable life and invite the power of God to change everything.

I believe one of the reasons Joshua, Elisha, Jabez, and so many other extraordinary persons in the Bible saw their boldest prayers answered was because they had no plan B. God's intervention was their everything. Their only hope.

How often do we pray, asking God for one thing, yet in the back of our minds think *"well if God doesn't do this, I can always just..."*. I know I do this. I pray half-heartedly. I hedge my bets because I want to avoid being disappointed in God. But what if this isn't prayer as God intended? What if when Jesus said "Ask and it will be given to you" He meant it (Matthew 7:7).

Why don't we pray like our lives depend on it? Because we're living lives that don't depend on God. More God would be nice. More *you fill in the blank* might be helpful. But if God doesn't intervene, if we neglect to pray – things will still be manageable.

I don't know about you, but I'm done with manageable. I want extraordinary. I want a faith-filled, no plan B, miracle-worthy kind of life. And that begins with faith-filled, no plan B, miracle-worthy kind of prayers.

Habit 3: Tithe From A Place Of Authority

When I worked at the local university, I started in the library department. Over time, I was given more responsibility over different academic support services. First, the computer labs. Second, tutoring services. Third, a grant-funded math program. And fourth, testing and assessment. I worked hard and did my best to keep up with my growing plate of duties, but eventually, I started to crack. I forgot assignments, missed meetings, and began to feel a mountain of stress every time I pulled into the university parking lot. I didn't know what to do. It felt like there was no way out.

My boss saw the stress on my face and called a meeting to find out what was going on. I told him the responsibilities had become too much and that I was stretched too thin. What he did next surprised me. He asked me whether or not I was in charge over these departments. Confused, because I wasn't sure where he was heading with this, I answered yes – I was the one in charge. I'll never forget what he said next.

It sounds to me like you've taken on all the responsibility of the position, but haven't used the authority of your position.

I was overwhelmed by responsibility because I was neglecting the authority that came along with it. This is the problem I see throughout the Christian sphere and most evidently when it comes to the issue of tithing.

When viewed from the perspective of responsibility, tithing seems like something we have to do. A necessary sacrifice for the obedient Christian. For those of us strapped for cash, trying to slowly climb out of debt and provide a half-decent life for our families – it almost seems like too much. Ten percent of not much leaves me with even less than not much! But this is only one perspective.

The other perspective, and the one I believe Scripture wants us to adopt, is that tithing is both a reminder and a confirmation of our access to divine authority.

In my university position, I began using my authority to reframe my responsibilities. I delegated more, rearranged meetings to fit my schedule, and strategically said no to some duties so that I could focus on what was most important. My responsibilities didn't go away. Rather, I was better able to fulfill my responsibility because I tapped into my authority.

In the same way, tithing was never meant to be a stress-inducing, financial chain Jesus wanted you to carry around your neck. It was meant to free us to be bold, expectant, and magnetic. Malachi 3:10 and Luke 6:38 both tell us to give, to tithe, and to expect a big return for our obedience! The Malachi verse even records God saying "test me in this."

Tithing is about so much more than money. As we give, we acknowledge God's authority over us and recognize the authority He has given us. God shared His authority with Jesus. Jesus shared His authority with the Holy Spirit. The Holy Spirit shares His authority with us. This authority grants us access to power, abundance, and so much more. It solidifies our new identity and perpetuates our new mindset.

As we shift our tithe from a necessary responsibility to a habit of authority, we will see a shift in our lives (and most definitely in our finances) as well. *Remember: Whoever sows sparingly will also reap sparingly, and whoever sows generously will also reap generously. 2 Corinthians 9:6*

Habit 4: Give Your Need

This first unfamiliar habit builds off of the previous habit of tithing. Giving takes many forms throughout Scripture. In the Old Testament, we see five main types of offerings: burnt, grain, peace, sin, and guilt. When including the New Testament, some scholars simplify this into just two categories: sin offerings and thanksgiving offerings. These are the motivations for giving. What the people actually gave varied widely as well: animals, food, money, rituals (gifts of time), and more. For this habit, I want to offer you some direction in how you can give purposefully above the tithe in today's context.

Kris Vallotton is pastor at Bethel Church in California and has one of the best stories I've heard for illustrating this principle.[xiii] A few years into his new role as a pastor (he was previously a business owner), he felt God calling him and his wife to pray for their mortgage to be completely paid off. Now, this was a tall order. They owed hundreds of thousands of dollars on their house (real estate isn't cheap in California!) and, if they stretched their budget, could maybe have it paid off in under a decade. Kris went to his wife and she said she had felt a similar urge as well. So they began praying together.

A few weeks into their praying, they got another prompting. This time to seek out a particular couple and pay their monthly mortgage payment for them. Again, not a small request! Kris and his wife had no idea how much that might be or if the couple would even let them do it. And on top of it all, wasn't this counterproductive to eliminating their own mortgage debt? Yet, Kris and his wife followed through and obeyed the prompting they felt had been Spirit-led. After multiple discussions, the couple finally agreed to let Kris make their payment. So he did and then...

Nothing. For months, nothing happened. Kris and his wife didn't feel any more promptings, even though they continued to pray daily for God's intervention – and also continued to aggressively pay their mortgage by strapping their budget. The Vallotton's were not going to give up, but they definitely wondered if what they had heard from God was accurate.

Then, long after they paid someone else's mortgage payment, and even longer after they had felt God's prompting to pray for their mortgage to be gone, something happened. Kris finished speaking at an event when a man he had never met walked right up to him, shook his hand, and said: "I think God told me to pay off your mortgage."

Kris was stunned. It's one thing to hope God will show up. It's a very different thing to actually see it happening! It turns out, this man was very wealthy and had been praying for a specific increase in his own life as well. So just like the couple was a means for Kris and his wife to give their need in faith, Kris's mortgage was this man's means.

The rest of the story reads like the happy ending of a movie plot. Within 30 days of their meeting, the man paid off Kris's mortgage, and two weeks after that sent Kris a picture of how God had answered his own prayer.

When I first came across this story, my jaw dropped to the floor. *I've never heard anything like that?* And then my skeptical mind asked, *is this even Biblical?* I began doing my research and I found two things.

1. Dozens of stories just like this one retold in testimonials across the web and even within my own network of church friends.
2. Biblical evidence that giving towards someone else's version of your specific need can be a powerful way of inviting God to work.

Let me share three short Biblical examples of what I mean. First, in Genesis 41 we see Joseph interpreting Pharaoh's dream. On the surface, this doesn't seem like giving since Joseph didn't need any dreams interpreted. However, there is so much more going on. Remember, Joseph wasn't summoned from some beach resort to come and help Pharaoh. He was called out of the prison cell he was thrown in unfairly and then forgotten by the man he helped get out. Joseph could have been angry, disgruntled, and refused to help Pharaoh. But instead, he chose to show him grace (*Gift 1*) and when offered the role of advisor, accepted the position to help fulfill Pharaoh's dream (*Gift 2*). Joseph received the second highest job in the land, along with all the perks of being one of Pharaoh's elite staff. The only explanation for this is grace *(Gift 1)*. Then, a few years into the famine Joseph witnessed his brothers bowing down before him – a fulfillment of the dream he had as a young boy and a "reward" for *Gift 2*.

The next story from 1 Kings 17 is simpler. Elijah is sent to an unnamed woman we only know as the widow of Zarephath. Hungry from traveling, Elijah asks the widow for food to which she replies: *I only have enough for one more meal for my son and I, then we will die* (1 Kings 17:12). But Elijah pushes her to make him the bread anyways. She makes the bread, feeds Elijah, and receives this word from the man of God: "*The jar of flour will not be used up and the jug of oil will not run dry until the day the Lord sends rain on the land.*" (v.14) The woman lacking food gave what food she had and never went hungry again.

The final story is one you have heard before: the feeding of the 5,000. In this story, which is captured by all 4 of the Gospel writers, we see a gigantic need and very few resources. But there is one detail which only the Gospel of John captures. All 4 Gospels mention the 5 loaves and 2 fish, but only John adds who they belonged to: "Here is a boy…" (John 6:9). In Matthew, Mark, and Luke the miracle focuses upon Jesus transforming very little into more than enough. In John, I think he wants us to remember the boy. To see how one small character surrendered his ability to meet his own need (I'm sure the boy was hungry too) so that God could meet a much bigger need through him. With faith like that, I can only imagine the life that boy must have lived!

You have the same opportunity as all of these stories. What is your most pressing need right now? Can you give towards someone else's mortgage, student loans, or medical debt? Can you give a sacrifice of time, energy, or peace so God can multiply your offering? Will you invite God to miraculously meet your need by meeting the needs of another?

Habit 5: Altar-Building To Remember

Today, when we study spiritual disciplines we examine habits like solitude, worship, reflection, and service. All of these are excellent actions to learn, but there is one discipline, or habit, I see repeatedly throughout Scripture that is practically absent from our modern faith context. That discipline is remembrance.

In the Old Testament, we see examples like building structures, hosting festivals, and offering sacrifices as a means of remembering what God did in some specific situation or how he answered prayer. In the New Testament, we are urged to remember the teachings of Jesus (Acts 20:35) and practice communion as a means of "remembrance" (Luke 22:19). God intended our faith to need refueling along the way, and through my study of the Bible, I believe the most effective way to practice the discipline of remembering is through something I call altar-building.

Altars are something we mainly see in the Old Testament. The word, altar, means to sacrifice or slaughter.[xiv] Furthermore, the altars on record are typically built with "stone, earth, metal, and brick." As the concept develops across the Bible, altars take on different forms and purposes. All kinds of sacrifices were accepted as a means of solving a multitude of both practical and religious concerns. My goal in sharing this information with you is not to bog you down with all the details of what altars were, but instead to show you how you can use them in your life right now. In order to accomplish this, I want to show you three Biblical examples from the book of Genesis.

First, in Genesis 12 we witness one of the first altars in the Bible. Abraham has just set out after receiving a word from God. Without clear direction or many details at all, Abraham trusted God for everything and blindly set out on the path in front of him. His travels brought him to a beautiful land that was inhabited by an entire nation at the time. Yet God met Abraham and told him, *To your offspring, I will give this land* (Genesis 12:7). It was an overwhelming promise. Abraham knew how time and life have a way of whittling away our beliefs in the promises of God, so he built something. He built an altar to God as a way of remembering what God had promised. Something he could see, touch, and hold when his faith grew weak. A physical reminder of what was yet to come.

In Genesis 26 we see Abraham's son, Isaac, build another altar. After a series of exhausting trials (conflict with the king of the Philistines, conflict with the local herders, and multiple major moves for his entire family and flocks), Isaac finally catches a break. He travels to a well his father had built many years ago and there encounters

God: *"I am the God of your father Abraham. Do not be afraid, for I am with you; I will bless you and will increase the number of your descendants for the sake of my servant Abraham."* With his faith refueled, Isaac builds an altar. A physical declaration of his renewed trust in God.

Finally, in Genesis 33 we see one more altar built. This time by Abraham's grandson and one of Isaac's sons: Jacob. Jacob has just survived the dreaded meeting with his twin brother Esau. Miraculously, Esau has forgiven Jacob for all the wrongs he experienced when they were younger. Jacob, slowly but surely, has become a man of God; abandoning his natural tendency to deceive and trading it for Godly trust. It's in this attitude that Jacob forgoes the opportunity to benefit from his brother's success and instead buys his own small plot of land and there builds an altar called *El Elohe Israel*: mighty is the God of Israel (Genesis 33:20).

From these examples, we can set some criteria for our own altars.

1. Altars should be physical/tangible reminders of something God has said or done.
2. Altars should be oriented around a promise: either something God has done or will do.
3. Altars should remind us of one of God's character traits.

In my own life, I have built up a small collection of altars to remind myself of all that God has done, and that I can look to when my faith needs a reminder of what God can do. In the top drawer of my bedroom dresser sits a picture of me on my last day in the hospital after battling a mysterious illness for months on end. It reminds me that God is my healer, that my body is His to protect, and that God alone determines the length of my earthly life.

On page 792 of my NIV Study Bible is the verse Psalm 16:7 "I will praise the LORD, who counsels me; even at night my heart instructs me." Above the verse are two dates and times when God woke me up in the middle of the night and led me directly to this verse (*July 20, 2009 at 4:53am and July 21, 2017 at 4:50am*). This altar reminds me that my path has always been, and will always be, in the gracious hands of God. When I feel lost or stuck or just plain confused, I pull this one out and remember Who is watching out for me.

The last altar I want to share with you is a $20 bill I have tucked in an envelope beside a small note which reads "God always provides." During one particularly stressful Sunday, when I was zoning out from the sermon because I didn't know how I was going to pay for my next semester of college, the pastor walked up to me (this is what happens when you sit in the front row), pulled out a $20 bill and asked "Will you trust Him?". As you could imagine, that event shook me to my core. I never forgot that day or how God provided for my school expenses. And I'll never get rid of that bill because I want to remember that my God is Lord over all abundance and through Him, I will always be provided for.

Your altar could be any number of things, representing all sorts of promises. To begin, I urge you to choose something meaningful God has already done in your life and build/choose an "altar" to remember it by. Then, going forward, be mindful of how you can incorporate altars into your walk with God. What things can help you remember what God has done as well as fuel your faith for what God can do? This is an exceptionally powerful habit and one I promise will ignite your faith to new levels.

Habit 6: Make Room Through Fasting

In Judges 7 we read about Gideon preparing to attack the Midian camp to the north. They've prepared for weeks for this encounter. Gideon received multiple signs from God that he would receive favor during the battle. Everything is lined up and ready to go until verse 2 when God throws a wrench into the entire plan: *Gideon...you have too many men.*

I'm no strategist, but it seems to me more men would be better when it came to ancient warfare. But God had something else in mind. Over the next 5 verses, God moves Gideon to whittle down his army of over 22,000 men to just 300. About 1% of the army's original size. With this small group of men, Gideon marched to the Midian camp and secured a decisive victory despite the overwhelming odds.

What does this story have to do with fasting? We'll get to that. But first, I want you to see that there is a pattern throughout Scripture of God calling His people to give up certain things before a breakthrough or victory can occur.

Abraham was willing to sacrifice Isaac. Esther was ready to sacrifice her own life. The Israelite men underwent circumcision, a sacrifice of flesh. Ruth gave up her home. David surrendered his chance to kill Saul. Gideon lost his army. Jesus gave everything.

And on the other side of every single one of their sacrifices – God showed up big! Abraham's descendants grew exponentially. Esther saved a nation. Israel conquered the Promised Land. Ruth gained a family and a place in history. David secured a kingdom for generations to come. Gideon became a hero. And Jesus gained everything.

Loss and gain are inextricably linked in God's order of things. Surrender invites victory. Sacrifice invites abundance.

Often, it seems God wants to remind us who the true source is for the good in our lives, and He does this by removing the "means" we think our blessing or promise or hope is supposed to come through. How can you win a war without an army? How can you have a family line if you sacrifice your only son? How can you usher in a new kingdom by letting the enemy kill you on a cross?

It doesn't make sense, and yet, this is the avenue God chooses again and again throughout the Bible. *Surrender to Me the logical way for it to happen and watch me do something else so that I alone receive the glory.*

In our everyday lives huge, life-altering sacrifices are rarely options we will face. Most of us will not have the opportunity to risk our life going against the ruling power like Esther or be called to offer our child to God like Abraham. However, we will face seemingly impossible sacrifices: like surrendering a job we're not sure how to provide for our family without, or moving to a place where we don't know anyone, or sacrificing our time to lead a ministry we feel profoundly unqualified to be in charge of. For these instances, the practice of "giving up" can be useful – and this is where fasting comes in.

The typical way we think about fasting is that it is a practice of abstaining from food for a certain period of time. This is true, but also incomplete. I like to think of fasting as *seasons of surrender*. First of all, you can fast from any good/helpful/productive activity in your life: eating food, watching television or reading fiction, hobbies, ministry duties, and even certain thought-patterns. Second, fasting is less about getting rid of something and more about making room for something else. Third, fasting is not about emptying your expectations. Instead, it's about recharging your expectations to look fully, aggressively, and persuasively in the direction of God.

Fasting prepares us for what can be by reworking our relationship with what is. I have found it useful to practice some form of fasting when you have a specific desire or timeline you are bringing to God. This practice of "surrender" can look different from person to person. Things I've fasted from include: food, computer games, leadership, sex, music, writing, and spending money. Each of these items was brought to mind by prayer or counsel from other Godly men and women. The length of these fasts lasted between 3 days and 3 months (the extent of the fast obviously depends on what you are fasting from).

Now, during these seasons of surrender, I used the time/energy/money not spent and redirected them towards other avenues God showed me. When I fasted from spending, I felt a conviction to reallocate that money to my local church. When I fasted from sex with my wife, I tackled some persistent issues of lust. When I fasted from leadership, I continued to serve but God used that time to build patience and humility in my spirit.

When I came out on the other end of these seasons (not always immediately, but definitely soon after) I reaped rewards for my efforts: my finances and marriage were blessed, and I was brought into an even higher position of leadership. These short fasts built in me tolerance for surrender. A tolerance that was called upon when greater challenges arose – like losing jobs, friends, and sacrificing things I believed were essential to where God was taking me.

Fasting, surrender, sacrifice – these are the means by which God accomplishes in His upside-down kingdom. Whereas our world thrives upon taking, gathering, and hoarding. God's kingdom flourishes when God's people open their hands: give, release, and offer. Because open hands are exactly what He is looking for so that He can fill them with even better things.

Habit 7: Affirmations of Divine Truth

Your life will move in the direction of your words. – Joel Osteen

U p to this point, we've covered habits which included both spiritual disciplines (Bible study, prayer) and practical actions (tithing, giving, altar-building, and fasting). This final habit is an action, a discipline, and a central component of *the triangle of what controls you*.

Words are one of the most powerful forces on earth. They have the ability to impact things we see: like our emotions and physical health. They also have the ability to impact things we cannot see: like our spirits and mental health. God sparked creation through His words, and on the last day, His words will determine the fate of every living thing.

Words carry the power of life and death, yet we tend to throw them around without much thought. I know I used to say things I regretted all the time, and these little blunders betrayed a deeper belief I didn't want to face – that I didn't actually believe my words had power. As long as that belief was in place, it became true. My words didn't have power. At their best, they described situations I felt I had no authority to change. At their worst, they perpetuated my unhelpful and even destructive behaviors and pushed away the *better* God had for me.

But eventually, I saw differently. I took a risk and began to be mindful of my words. More than that, I began to use them proactively rather than reactively. I wanted to bring life through my words instead of death and I knew the Bible would show me how.

This is where affirmations come in. Using words correctly to create the life you desire is much too important and complex a subject to lump in with another concept. Although affirmations are one of the *Magnetic Habits*, they are also so much more. I urge you to keep reading because you have almost completely unlocked how to rewrite *the triangle of what controls you* so that you can control it, and therefore, attract the best God has been waiting to give you!

Form Follows Function

There's a phrase in the architecture and design communities that says "form follows function." One definition of this phrase is that "the shape of a building or object should primarily relate to its intended function or purpose."[xv] Let me simplify it a little further. When you are building something from scratch or creating something new, there's a process involved. And for anyone who is a creator of some type, whether you are a writer, baker, artist, carpenter, construction worker, and so on – you know that with any new project, there can be multiple "good" places to begin. The "form follows function" phrase aims to guide us towards the best starting point: what is the object's purpose?

If you can know the *why* of what you are building, then the other pieces should fall into place. For example, if you are making a camouflage hat, you're probably not going to use bright pink as one of your colors. If you are making a boot that will last in the winter snow, it should probably be waterproof. And you likely don't need to spend a lot of time figuring out how it can help people run faster. The function of the object takes priority. What was it made to do? Why does it matter? And then, once those questions are answered, you can focus on perfecting the form: the look, shape, and feel. This doesn't mean that form is less important than function. It means that the best form is one which enables and supports function.

So how does this relate?

The function (or why) of *Magnetic Faith* is to equip you to become everything God intended you to be so that you could attract, attain, and accomplish everything that God has for you. The form (or how) of *Magnetic Faith* is the set of tools and concepts we have learned throughout this series.

Form follows function.

If you try to keep your attention focused on the what (blessings you will attract) and how (form) rather than the why (function), you'll end up missing the boat every time. I can't tell you what transforming your identity, mindset, habits, and words will lead to. But I can promise that they will lead to something and somewhere beyond your imagination!

The look, shape, and feel of your best life depends upon you committing to function the way God intended using the forms I have shown you. To walk in power, to think with authority, and to act with expectation. When your *Godly-why* becomes your center, your God-ordained *what* becomes inevitable.

You have made immense progress by making it this far, and now you only have a little further to go. It's time to bring everything you have learned together and truly unlock the magnetism you were meant for. Now we must explore the entity of life and death. It's time to close the triangle and discover the power of *Magnetic Words*.

How to Create and Control Your Habits

In my opinion, habits are the "tipping point" of the *Magnetic Faith* process. If you can implement these with the appropriate foundations in place (i.e. your identity and mindset), significant changes in your life are sure to follow. May you have all the courage and strength to take the next step.

1. **Finish The Series.** You, my friend, are almost there! And so once more I must urge you to continue reading. Although *Magnetic Habits* may sit atop the triangle, the structure is not yet complete. The final section will bring everything we have learned together and fully equip you to make the changes you most desire by activating the faith you already have access to. Your persistence in this journey speaks volumes about your character and about your commitment to pursuing real transformation. I hope you see that and are encouraged to finish

strong!

2. **Take A Habit Inventory.** Entrepreneur and author Gary Vaynerchuk writes that "Self-awareness is your most important attribute." You won't know what needs to change until you are honest about what is going on. This is something I thought I was pretty good at...until I got married. Then, all of a sudden, I had another human being around me 24 hours a day, 7 days a week. My wife (lovingly) began to call out all sorts of bad habits I honestly had no idea were taking place. They were so ingrained in my pattern of life that I was blind to them. But once she helped me become aware of what was going on, that gave me the momentum I needed to change.

You may or may not have someone in your life who could be the "up-close and personal awareness guard" you need to get started. Either way, here are some steps to get you headed in the right direction.

   I. Commit to taking a habit inventory over the next 3 days.
   II. In a journal or notebook, make 2 categories: *Habits I Want To Keep* and *Habits I Want To Stop*.
   III. Every 3 hours (yes, this often), pull out the notebook and review what has gone on during those last few hours – placing

> the actions you engaged in under either of the categories.
>
> IV. Continue this for the full 3 days.

I guarantee you will discover actions and patterns you never knew existed. That is the first step to lasting change. The second step is figuring out ways to eliminate the bad habits and replace them with magnetic ones. Do you tend to waste time on social media when you are bored? Is there a way you can purposely seek out the needs of others during that time instead? Do you scan through junk articles online? Could you set up a Bible reading plan in its place? Be creative yet aggressive. Your current habits created the life you now live. If you want something different, then you must act differently.

3. **Start Ridiculously Small.** One of my favorite writers, Leo Babauta, deserves the credit for this idea. In an article explaining how to actually stick to habits, he wrote:

Another common habit that too few people actually do is flossing daily. So my advice is just floss one tooth the first night. Of course, that seems so ridiculous most people laugh. But I'm totally serious: if you start out exceedingly small, you won't say no. You'll feel crazy if you don't do it. And so you'll actually do it! That's the point. Actually doing the habit is much more important than how much you do.[xvi]

I love this concept because you can apply it to any of the *Magnetic Habits* we covered above. Instead of committing to read your Bible in a year, leave your Bible open on a desk or table and commit to just looking at it once a day. That might seem ridiculous – but that's the point. It's so ridiculous you're almost guaranteed to do it, even by accident. And walking by an open Bible might lead you to read a single verse, which may lead to reading a chapter, and so on. As Leo said, actually engaging in the habit is more important than how much of it you do.

4. **Revisit Your Wants.** In the closing section of *Magnetic Identity*, one of the exercises was to write down a list of your desires and how your God-given identities could relate to each one. For this last practical step, I want you to revisit that list and take it one step further. Choose any 3 of the desires from your list and figure out which of the *Magnetic Habits* covered above you could use to achieve that particular desire. If you are asking God for a miracle – is there an altar you can build to remember the miracles He has already given you? If you are praying for a house – is there a family you can make a mortgage payment for? If you are asking God for clarity – is there a Scripture you felt led to dive into? Approach this practical step with prayer and see what the Holy Spirit has to say. Remember, your expectations are the key!

By engaging in the habits of Bible reading, prayer, tithing, altar-building, need-giving, and fasting you are igniting both the spiritual authority and practical power of your *Magnetic Faith*. The *triangle of what controls you* is nearly under your control. You are consciously choosing the direction your life will go. Every piece of you is being reshaped into God's perfect design. Now you are ready for the next step.

Part 4: Magnetic Words

How To Use The Life-Changing Power Of Speaking God's Word

You Are Already Magnetic

There's a truth I've touched on along the way, but have held back from fully diving into. I needed you to understand the potential of magnetism before this truth could have its proper effect. In the previous parts, you learned pieces of the reality God intends for us to live in: identities He wants to define us, mindsets He wants to guide us, and habits He wants us to act on. These segments are part of God's grand plan to remake creation into everything it was originally meant to be.

Each part, when used correctly, attracts to it a distinct set of beneficial rewards. A magnetic identity, one shaped by Biblical truths, attracts to it the gifts and powers available to those who walk in God's truth. A magnetic mindset, one set on believing in God's abundant reality, attracts to it renewed vision and energy with which to act on. A commitment to magnetic habits, actions guided by Scriptural promises and Spiritual wisdom, attract to them an ever-increasing number of both practical and spiritual prizes.

However, the reality you must understand is that magnetism works both ways. In fact, you are already magnetic.

The life you have right now is a direct result of the things you have attracted into it. The identities you walk in, the mindsets you allow, the habits you engage in – all of these have come together to produce the life you currently live, for better or worse.

You are a magnet whether you realized it or not. But the good news is, the idea we've been building since page one, is that you can change what you attract. You can transform your magnetism from whatever it was, into everything God intended it to be.

In this final section of *Magnetic Faith*, you will learn exactly how to make the changes you desire. The transformation will not occur overnight and the work will require, quite literally, every part of you. Your identity, mindset, and habits must come into agreement. They must come together to form the triangle of God's design. And the only way to accomplish this is to activate the final piece: the life-changing power of speaking *Magnetic Words*.

The Tree, The Fruit and The Problem

Before we fully examine the scope and depth of the power of our words, I want to spend some time revisiting Scripture. The Bible is the starting place for every lasting change God desires us to make in our lives, and the starting point for every area we want to transform as well.

In order to utilize this tool in the way we need to, we first have to become familiar with it. In addition to making serious study of Scripture a regular part of our lives (as we talked about in *Magnetic Habits*), there are some themes we must learn, believe, and apply for our words to have their full effect.

Luke 6:43-45a

"No good tree bears bad fruit, nor does a bad tree bear good fruit. Each tree is recognized by its own fruit. People do not pick figs from thornbushes, or grapes from briers. A good man brings good things out of the good stored up

in his heart, and an evil man brings evil things out of the evil stored up in his heart."

The first theme we will look at is the Biblical idea of *heart*. In both the Old and New Testaments, the concept of the heart referred to more than just the organ inside one's body. When Biblical writers spoke about the heart, they were speaking about the very core of the person. The *source* of everything they were.

Sounds like something else we covered, right? When you read verses about the heart, I want you to exchange the word with *identity* and see how that changes or clarifies the meaning of the verse.

In Luke 6, we learn that the fruit we see on the tree was a result of the kind of tree it grew from. An apple tree could never produce coconuts and vice versa. In fact, in order to correctly identify a tree you wouldn't have to examine its roots or trunk or even its leaves. All you would have to do is reach up and see what kind of fruit is available.

These verses are telling us that it's just as easy for God to see what kind of person we really are. He knows our roots, trunks and leaves tell a story – but what He's looking for is *our fruit* because that's what others can see. It's our fruit that carries the potential to transform this world and our lives. And it's our fruit which reveals the most truth about who we really believe we are.

Our identity (our heart and core) brings specific things into our lives. Saying it produces certain fruit is the same thing as saying it attracts certain results.

Your identity is magnetic right now. Your innermost life produces the fruit you are known by, good or bad, edible or toxic.

Proverbs 23:7 (NKJV)

"For as he thinks in his heart, so is he."

The second theme both builds upon and confirms the first. In Proverbs 23, we get a varied list of wisdom sayings covering everything from not drinking too much wine to controlling your behavior around important company. About one-fifth of our way through the chapter is when we come across one of the most famous lines of Solomon: "as he thinks...so is he."

Notice the concept of heart is brought up again. The subject in this passage is not just thinking with his brain, but rather, he is thinking with his entire self. His thoughts are *coming up* from the depth of his being. This is our second theme: the connection between heart and mind.

Our modern age has made it a rule to separate things into their distinct parts. In college you choose a major and learn more and more about a smaller area of study. In medicine, you go to a different specialist depending on which part of your body is experiencing pain. Even in the gym, there are different machines for every muscle you could think of exercising. We've grown so accustomed to compartmentalizing our world that we've lost how interconnected everything actually is.

This is one reason why holistic medicine has grown such a strong following. Often the way to heal one part of the body is to focus on another. The concept of interconnectedness was built into the very fabric of our being (both physical and spiritual) and when we neglect it, we profoundly miss everything God has for us.

Your thoughts are a product of the mindsets you have chosen to allow which are fueled by the identities you have adopted as your own. Your whole self is ONE self. Your identity, mindset, habits and words are united. They intertwine and influence one another. You cannot carry around a renewed mind and continue in destructive habits any more than a fig tree can grow pears.

As a person thinks in their heart, so are they. Completely, entirely.

But...and this is a big BUT. As a person changes, so *can* they be.

Galatians 6:3-4a, 7

"If anyone thinks they are something when they are not, they deceive themselves. Each one should test their own actions... Do not be deceived: God cannot be mocked. A man reaps what he sows."

The third and final theme we will address concerns our tendency to deceive ourselves. Galatians, like many of Paul's letters, is communal. Its main aim is to address the problems he sees are tearing the community apart. So much of what it means to be Christian can only be accomplished with other human beings – but that's a discussion for another time.

Here, Paul addresses a problem we often see in our own lives: people's actions aren't aligning with who they claim to be. Paul begins the discussion with the mind: "If anyone thinks..." Paul intimately understands the connectedness of human identity, thoughts, and actions. He knows that the problems he is trying to address (people's unhelpful or inappropriate actions) are just a symptom of a deeper issue.

But since people can't pull out their heart or mind and set it on a table to examine what's wrong, Paul offers us a different solution. We must examine the fruit of these entities; what we actually *reap*.

When God set the world into motion, He put a definite order in place. The waters could only come so far. The night would only last so long. And seeds could only grow what they were designed to grow. Farmers knew this principle so when they planted wheat, they expected a wheat harvest (*like begets like*). This was the rhythm God ordained.

In the same way, the actions we engage in represent both ends of the system. On one hand, they are the product of what we have sowed internally. We reap productive or destructive habits depending upon what has been sown into our deepest selves. On the other hand, actions are what we sow into the world so that we can reap physical, tangible results. Like seeds, actions always follow the rhythm of like-begets-like.

This is where the third theme comes to light: any single malfunctioning area in our magnetic faith triangle reveals that the entire structure is damaged.

Everything is connected. Every area influences another. And so if we don't like what we are seeing or experiencing in any one area, it's not enough to just bandage that part. The entire structure has to be addressed. Deep work has to be done. Either all of the *Magnetic Faith* pieces work together or none of them work at all.

This might sound a bit harsh, but I need you to get this idea before we move any further. The life you want, the life filled with God's best, will require more of you than you have ever been willing to give before. It will ask you to dig deeper and stretch further than you thought possible.

All of this is necessary to rewire your magnet. All of this is essential to activating the power that has been lying dormant within.

4 Rules For Holy Living

Here are the three themes we covered once more:

1. Your heart, or core, represents your identity. From it everything flows, but you can choose what it is made of.
2. Every part of yourself (and *the triangle of what controls you*) is interconnected. Every piece influences the other.
3. Either the entire structure works or none of it does. Any single malfunctioning area reveals damage throughout.

With these three in mind, let's revisit Colossians 3 so that we can begin to understand the triangle at a deeper level.

In my NIV Study Bible, Colossians 3 has a subtitle above the chapter which reads "Rules for Holy Living." At one time in my faith walk, I would have steered away from this. I thought Christianity was about freedom – why would I want to start adding a bunch of rules to my life?

As I matured, my understanding developed. I started to see that rules and boundaries are actually the pathway to freedom. God gave us rules not so that He could *keep us* from what is good, but so that we could make ourselves *available* for what is good.

This is the intention of Colossians 3 – to help us make our entire selves available, open, prepared to accept God's best. More than that, Colossians 3 gives us the tools needed to attract God's best.

Below are the rules, as I understand them, present in Colossians 3. I have laid them out for you plainly, along with their Biblical support, so that you could fully grasp the powerful truths they hold.

To have a holy life and a magnetic faith:

Rule 1: You must accept your radically new identity.

- 3:1 You have been raised...you heart (or core) is set on higher things.
- 3:3 Your life (existence, purpose, direction) is inextricably linked to Christ and His mission.
- 3:11 Your old identifying markers (race, gender, status) have fallen away and your new markers (power, freedom, life) are dominant.

Rule 2: You must adopt the higher thoughts of your Heavenly Father.

- 3:2 Your mindset has to shift from what you see as possible (earthly things) to what God says is possible (things above).
- 3:10 Your knowledge, understanding of the world and how it works, is being renewed (changed and upgraded) by the Bible.
- 3:15 Your mind is ruled by peace because of what God has revealed to you.

Rule 3: You must choose to engage in life-producing actions.

- 3:5 Walk away from the actions which claimed to have power over you.
- 3:12 Put on actions motivated by your new self, your new understanding, and your new power.
- 3:14 Let the love you have received from God, the love you have for others, and the love you have for yourself, guide every activity.

Rule 4: Your words are the binding force of transformation, you must use them for life and not death.

- 3:8 You must *rid yourself* of dead words and powerless language.
- 3:9 Do not lie because all of you has been reshaped by truth.
- 3:16 Let your words be full of wisdom for teaching, encouragement for people, joy for praise, and gratitude towards God.

These rules are the pathway to a magnetic faith. The essence of a holy life. The keys to unlocking God's best in the here and now.

How Our Words Work

I have spent so much time readdressing the structure and interconnectedness of the *Magnetic Faith* triangle because words serve a unique role in its structure.

As you can see in the drawing above, the first three parts build upon one another. Identity sits first near the bottom, mindset sits in the middle, and habits rest on top. It would make sense for words to be a very small piece at the very top of the structure, but through my study of the Bible I discovered something different.

Rather than simply being another part of the escalating structure, words play a much more important role. They bind the structure together. Without words, there is no triangle!

In Scripture, we read about the power of God's spoken words. In Psalm 33:6 we read, "By the word of the LORD the heavens were made." Everything we see in creation was first a word. God spoke and from the power of His words – where there was nothing – something came to be.

John 1 continues this theme. "In the beginning was the Word, and the Word was with God, and the Word was God." John begins his gospel on a bold note. He declares that Jesus is God, but he does it in a clever way. He elevates Jesus from the human teacher and prophet to the very Word of God. John presents his readers with an eternal perspective of Jesus. And more than that, he begins to empower his readers at the same time.

Just as Jesus came and had power because of the Word of God. We too, God's chosen people, have been remade by the Word of God. God spoke our new selves into being, and by doing so, imbued us with some of His same power.

Now to move one step further, Colossians 1 reveals to us two properties of God's spoken power. The first is that God's Word has the power to create, "all things have been created through him and for him" (v.16). We've already established this truth with Psalm 33, but we could also reach back to Genesis or Job or Isaiah to solidify this point. The second point, and the one which directly ties into our triangle structure, is found in Colossian 1:17, "and in him all things hold together."

If we take the truth in Colossians 1:17 and pair it with the truth in John 1 we begin to see that the Word of God, God's spoken truth, Jesus' power, not only creates new things but is responsible for holding these new things together in their proper shape.

This is the same power we have as God's children and as co-heirs with Christ. Our words have power, not just in a general sense, but the power to accomplish specific things within God's world.

First, our words have the power to create.

Second, our words have the power to hold together.

This is why we had to save *Magnetic Words* for the very end. Everything you have learned along the way has prepared you for these coming lessons. Going forward, you will learn how to access the power you already have to both create and hold together your magnetic faith. But you should also know that by learning this information, you are now responsible. Responsible for creating and securing the identities, mindsets, and habits you were meant to walk in.

Biblical Ammunition For Your Power

Accepting that your words have actual, tangible, effectual power both in the physical and spiritual realm can be a lot to take in, especially if you haven't been exposed to this truth before. To help equip you for this, I want to show you a selection of verses taken straight from the Bible which support this idea. I want you to not only *know* that you have this power but *believe* you do as well. Because this is the only way you'll take the courageous action needed to transform your life.

Your words can literally bring about life and death.

- (Proverbs 18:21) Death and life are in the power of the tongue...
- (Proverbs 15:4) The soothing tongue is a tree of life...
- (Proverbs 12:18) ...the tongue of the wise brings healing.

Your words are both a product of who you are and the producer of who you are.

- (Matthew 15:18) But what comes out of the mouth proceeds from the heart, and this defiles a person.
- (Mathew 12:37) For by our words you will be justified, and by your words you will be condemned.
- (Luke 6:45) The good person out of the good treasure of his heart produces good, and the evil person out of his evil treasure produces evil, for out of the abundance of the heart his mouth speaks.

Your words create your life, for better or worse.

- (Proverbs 18:20) From the fruit of their mouth a person's stomach is filled; with the harvest of their lips they are satisfied.
- (Proverbs 21:23) Those who guard their mouths and their tongues keep themselves from calamity.
- (James 3:2, 4-6) Anyone who is never at fault in what they say is perfect, able to keep their whole body in check... Take ships as an example. Although they are so large and are driven by strong winds, they are steered by a very small rudder wherever the pilot wants to go. Likewise, the tongue is a small part of the body...[but it] sets the whole course of one's life.

Your words are a tool with which you can create or destroy, build up or tear down, attract or repel. You have been utilizing their power your entire life, whether you realized it or not. All that matters now is what you will do next.

Breathe

Okay... pause.

Take a minute.

I know, some of these concepts and truths seem to be rushing out at the speed of sound. I probably could have taken more time to explain these. To stretch them out and illustrate them with more stories.

But the truth is no matter how I present them, whether they come through a thousand-page book or on the back of a notecard... they're true.

Your WORDS have power.

YOU have power.

And that excites me! It's exciting because I know what this power can do, the way it can transform a life. Scripture shows us what can happen when we believe that God gives His children, His chosen people, power.

Amazing things. Unbelievable things. Little becomes much. Dead dreams live again. Things that seemed impossible become inevitable.

This is what you are tapping into. This is what you are working towards.

Greater things (John 14:12).

This is why you must finish as strongly as you began.

Your words are both the last piece and the first step on your journey towards an undeniably, unrelenting, *Magnetic Faith*.

Are you ready? ...I think you are.

The 3 Magnetic Affirmations

In the English language, there are just over 170,000 unique words. If you count derivatives, compound words, and other variations that number balloons to nearly 600,000.[xvii]

We have no shortage of words.

But the number of words you know or use does not directly correlate to their power. In Matthew 6, Jesus gives us a profound insight not only into the practice of prayer – but into the practice of using powerful words.

"Do not keep on babbling...they think they will be heard because of their many words." (Matthew 6:7)

So if it's not the *number* of words we use which activate our God-given authority that means the power must lie in the *type* of words we use. At the very end of this book, I will include a Recommended Reading List which contains multiple titles on the subject of words. These can help as you discover which words are worth keeping, and which can fall out of your vocabulary.

For now, in this book, I want to give you 3 simple sets of affirmations which will bring everything we have learned together and secure the triangle you have been building along the way. These affirmations, although unassuming, carry immense influence when used correctly. They are the catalysts for both inner and outer transformation, and they are ready to be spoken by you.

Affirmation 1: I Am

These two simple words, "I am", have a powerful history throughout the Bible. When Moses asked God by what name should he free the Israelite people from their Egyptian rulers, God answered: I AM. (*Exodus 3*) When characters embarked upon their new callings and received new names, they confirmed their new destiny with these two words: *I am...*

> I am Abraham, not just Abram.
>
> I am Sarah, no long Sarai.
>
> I am Israel, Jacob is no more.
>
> I am Peter, I used to be Simon.
>
> I am Paul, Saul has been transformed.

In the Gospel of John, we even see Jesus take part in the power of this phrase. Seven times Jesus spoke an "I am" statement as a means of communicating His eternal status, temporal mission, and promised gift.

> I am the bread of life. (John 6:35)
>
> I am the light of the world. (John 8:12)

I am the gate. (John 10:9)

I am the good shepherd. (John 10:11)

I am the resurrection and the life. (John 11:25)

I am the way, the truth, and the life. (John 14:6)

I am the vine. (John 15:5)

What do we learn from these examples? First, "I am" statements were a means for the divine (God and Jesus) to confirm their identities and power. Second, "I am" statements were also used to communicate the promised (or soon-to-be) identities of humans.

In Exodus and John, God and Jesus share their truth through "I am" statements as a means of inviting people into their mission in the world. God was going to rescue the Israelites with or without Moses' help. But He chose to invite a human into his grand plan, and reveal a part of His character by doing so. In a similar way, Jesus came to save the world and had all the power to do so on his own. Yet he chose to include humans (the apostles and disciples) as a key part of that plan.

"I am" statements have embedded in them an invitational nature. When you proclaim that you are something, you are, to some degree, inviting someone else to see or benefit from that thing you are. If you say, "I am a good cook," those words stir a desire in the hearer to taste your food. If you say, "I am fast," that may present a challenge to the audience to see just how fast you really are.

In the same way, when Jesus says I am the light – we want to see how bright that light shines. Or when He says He is the good shepherd – we want to be taken care of. The "I am" statements of God should move us to want to see them played out before us and for us.

Therefore, if "I am" statements can communicate promised outcomes and have the power to invite – that means when we engage our magnetic faith by voicing "I am" statements, we actually invite God into our transformation (*promised outcome*). "I am" statements confirm in ourselves that we believe the thing we speak is possible. And at the same time, draw God in to make it possible.

The following seven statements are profoundly simple but do not overlook them because of that. Remember, the authority of these words does not lie in their complexity or number, but in their *type*. We have seen "I am" statements used by God's chosen people and even by God and Jesus themselves. Now it's time for us to utilize their power.

I am unique.

I am an heir.

I am new.

I am free.

I am destined.

I am loved.

I am powerful.

Later in this book, I will help you craft a strategy for integrating these statements into your daily life, and therefore, unlocking the ability they have to shape your magnetic faith triangle. For now, I just want to make you aware of what they are.

Take a minute now to repeat them aloud, slowly. Feel the power of each phrase. If you feel a tinge of doubt or resistance to them, that's okay. Our list of power words is not yet complete. As we continue to build your toolset your confidence will grow.

I want you to know that I believe you are these things, even if you don't yet. More than that, God believes these things for you. The great I AM wants you to accept everything you are.

Affirmation 2: I Believe

There is a slight, but vital difference between thoughts and belief. Thoughts come and go. They're fluid, temperamental, and often short-lived. Many times we get thoughts in our mind that we have no idea where they came from. Most importantly, the only relationship we have to some thoughts is that they happen to have entered our mind.

Beliefs are something more. Beliefs may begin as thoughts, whether our own or as we become exposed to the thoughts of others. What transforms a thought into a belief is the action of acceptance. Our relationship to the idea shifts. The concept or notion moves from being *a* thought to being *our* thought. We adopt a form of ownership around the thought and this upgrades into a belief.

Once a thought becomes a belief, that is when measurable changes occur. Beliefs never remain only in our heads. Every belief plays itself out in our lives to some degree – that is what separates them from thoughts. Thoughts come and go, and disappear like a mist. Beliefs grow down into the soil of our souls and reshape the direction of our lives.

That is why wrapping words around our beliefs is an essential practice. Every one of us has thoughts which have dug down into our deepest being and pulled our lives along for better or worse. But the true power is not merely in exposing your beliefs, but using your words to accept (or implant) new ones.

This is where the second set of affirmations come in.

For the first affirmation, the two words we focused on were "I am." For these declarations, we will be activating the power of two more words: "I believe."

In the Bible, the idea of belief and faith are inextricably linked so it's challenging to find verses or evidence relating to only one of these two words. However, there are a few short examples I think will help communicate this point.

First, we have the case of Abraham. In Romans 4, Paul references Genesis 15:6 when he writes, "Abraham believed God, and it was credited to him as righteousness." This powerful Scripture provides us with a perfect example of what I outlined above. God gave Abraham a thought: that he could still have a son even though he was very old. Abraham took the thought and accepted it, meaning he evaluated the source of the thought (God) and chose to move that idea into the category of belief. That action alone, simply mentally changing the category from thought to belief, so pleased God that He counted it as *righteousness*.

Righteousness is one of those words we might hear all the time in the Christian sphere, but what does it actually mean? And what did it matter for Abraham to have that label placed upon him? In Greek, that word literally means "one who is as he ought to be."[xviii]

Take that in for a second. Abraham didn't have a son yet. His wife wasn't pregnant. He hadn't taken any "tangible" action. And yet God looked at him and said *This one is right, good, acceptable, perfect.* Abraham's belief altered his status with God. As his status changed: blessing, opportunity, and promise became inevitable.

The second example I want to show you is taken from Matthew 9. In this chapter, Jesus heals a paralyzed man, raises the dead, and saves a bleeding woman. Then, in the last story in the chapter, two blind men find Jesus and ask him for mercy. In the previous three miracles, Jesus simply healed the hurting person and then sent them on their way. But here he does something different.

Before healing their blindness He asks them "Do you *believe* that I am able to do this?" Wasting no time, the two men reply "Yes Lord!" Jesus heals them and they thank him by disregarding his warning (he told them not to tell anyone, but they immediately do the opposite).

This scene always bothered me. Why did Jesus question their belief? Clearly, they believed or else they wouldn't have chased him across town yelling for him to pay attention to their need. The answer begins to emerge when you take a closer look at the chapter. In every other miracle, there were specific words exchanged. The leader voiced his specific belief and request in verse 18. The bleeding woman "said to herself" in verse 21 and confirmed her belief.

The two blind men used their initial words more generally. The only asked for "mercy." Perhaps this meant they believed Jesus could heal them, or maybe they didn't want to aim so high – so they made a more general request: *show me mercy Jesus, whatever that may be*.

But Jesus doesn't work with generalities. He wanted their specific belief and so he called them out. "Do you believe I am able to do *this."* Only after they voiced their specific belief did they receive the miracle.

In the same way, your words have the power to shift your standing with God and bring about miraculous results, but only when those words are specific and uttered aloud. As we did above, I now want to give you seven more magnetic words that you can use to build your belief muscle and unlock the mind (and thereby the miraculous life) God has reserved for you.

I believe in growth.

I believe in abundance.

I believe in progress.

I believe in God's timing.

I believe in focus.

I believe in authenticity.

I believe in God's support.

As you can see, these seven are also based off the seven mindsets previously addressed. If using "I am" statements invite God, using "I believe" statements ignite God. God loves to act on behalf of those who believe. Belief brings God joy. New beliefs reveal that our deepest transformation (our identity, heart, core) is starting to take root and impact our whole inner self.

But this revolution has to be spoken. Your beliefs must become words if they are going to activate the faith available to you, and move the God who is ready and able to help.

Affirmation 3: I Commit

Let me ask you a question. Are you merely interested in living the best life God has for you? Or are you committed?

Interested means you might be excited by the idea, but there are limits to what you are willing to give up in your pursuit of it. In fact, you'd be hard pressed to step outside your comfort zone.

Commitment is something else entirely. Commitment places uncomfortable, stretching demands upon your person. It grows out of something more than simple interest. Dr. Heidi Reeder, a communications researcher, defines commitment in this way: "Commitment is the experience of being psychologically attached to something and intending to continue."[xix]

Her research confirms what we have covered in this series. Our mindset (psychological attachment) influences our habits (or commitments). When I was developing the theory behind this book, I knew I had to choose a word which captured the full force of what magnetic words could accomplish in the area of our actions. Saying things like *I promise* or *I will* weren't strong enough. I knew there was a better term and that is when I stumbled upon our third and final affirmation: "I commit."

Once I decided this was exactly the phrase I wanted to communicate, I turned to Scripture for examples of commitment, but also for examples of how the word itself was used throughout the Bible. That's when I found something very interesting. Of the 152 times, the word "commit" and its variations are used, about 95% were used in the context of sin.

Oh, what a great sin these people have committed! (Ex. 32:21)

But a man who commits adultery has no sense; (Prov. 6:32)

The Lord will punish all those who commit such sins. (1 Thess. 4:6)

I almost abandoned the word until I realized the connection. Great sins require commitment, just as much as great successes do. A person doesn't just wake up one day and commit murder or have an affair. There's a process involved. At first, the person felt negative emotions. Over time, they let those feelings create scenarios in their minds. Then, at some point, the "psychological attachment" to these emotions and ideas played themselves out in a violent or passionate act of sin.

Multiple times along the way, the individual had an opportunity to stop. They could have confessed their feelings or chosen to think differently. But instead, they allowed their intention to continue to direct them all the way into destruction.

I know I have felt this process in my own heart and mind. The struggle to stop short of sin but letting myself go further than I ever wanted. We might not call that commitment, but that is how the Bible sees it. Whenever we count the reward for taking action as more valuable than the cost, we are engaging in the practice of commitment.

Commitment carves a path into our realities. Like we spoke about previously with our minds, once we allow certain thoughts in it becomes easier to think those thoughts again because of the worn pathways through our brains. Actions work the same way. We are more likely to continue down treaded pathways because our commitments (or habits) have laid out the easiest path forward.

But you, reading this right now, have a choice. What's the best way to destroy a destructive commitment? Make a *new* commitment. Look towards the direction you want to go. Voice your intention to get there and then take massive action on behalf of your newfound faith. That is the way forward and these seven commitment affirmations will help you get there.

I commit to taking my Bible seriously.

I commit to praying because my life depends on it.

I commit to tithe from authority.

I commit to regularly give my needs.

I commit to build altars to remember.

I commit to making intentional room through fasting.

I commit to continually speaking divine truth.

There's one more essential piece to this step. True commitments reduce (and even eliminate) choices. Dr. Reeder says that options can actually be the enemy of commitment because they offer us alternative paths and weaken our resolve to stick to the one we've chosen. In a world where "keeping your options open" is considered almost a divine right, this can be a difficult truth to stomach.

What do you want to commit to and why? What are you willing to endure? What are you willing to lose?

Your commitments will carry you anywhere you want to go, so long as you give yourself fully to them.

Never Empty

"We cannot be too careful about the words we use; we start out using them and they end up using us." — Eugene H. Peterson

Words are never an end unto themselves. We say things for a reason: to evoke emotion, make requests, share pain or praise, tell stories, and an endless number of more beautiful and terrible things. To believe that your words have lost all power is to lose all hope. The unvoiced story is the most painful. The untold truth is the heaviest to carry.

Words free us. They open the skylights of our souls and invite God in to do the work only he can do. Every time a word leaves our mouths, something changes. Something is moved or shaped, grown or broken.

As the rain and the snow come down from heaven, and do not return to it without watering the earth and making it bud and flourish, so that it yields seed for the sower and bread for the eater, so is my word that goes out from my mouth: It will not return to me empty, but will accomplish

what I desire and achieve the purpose for which I sent it. Isaiah 55:10-11

Maybe one of the reasons God speaks so rarely is because He understands the power of His words so deeply. Every word God utters shifts the fabric of the entire universe. Every phrase of His is like an ambassador sent on a mission. Each one accomplishes. Each one achieves.

What will it take for us to think about our words this way? That they are ambassadors of life or death we get to send out into the world. That our words have a life of their own. Lives that eventually form *our* lives in return.

I want you to be aware of what you are actually doing every time you open your mouth. That you, my friend and God's chosen, are bringing into reality the content of your communication. Your words are not empty. God has graced us with this responsibility and it is both my pleasure and burden to draw your attention to it.

Use the kinds of words you want to be used by. Words you would be proud to see displayed where all could see. Words that would bring honor, and not shame, if God had them laid out before His eyes.

The work is difficult but the rewards are immeasurable.

How The Three Work Together

There are numerous ways you can begin integrating these affirmations into your daily practice. To help guide you, I want to share 3 of my favorite methods.

1. **Recite all "I am" statements.**

The most important place to start is with the identity affirmations. As we've discussed before, these are the foundation for every change you want to see happen in and through your life. Start by writing all 7 magnetic word statements on a piece of paper or notecard and place them somewhere you will see daily. Then, every morning when you wake up and evening before you go to sleep recite the statements aloud.

This is a simple way to get yourself headed in the right direction. Over time, you'll become so familiar with the seven statements that you won't even have to look at your writing any longer. When that happens, I would suggest moving to one of these other practice types.

2. The ABC Method.

I honestly didn't plan for it to work this way, but when you look at the three statements covered a pattern emerges: I Am (A), I Believe (B), I Commit (C). In my notes, I started calling this the ABC's of transformation. For this practice, choose one statement from each of the three categories. For example: *I am an heir, I believe in abundance, I commit to tithe from authority*. You can create some truly powerful affirmations using this method. Here is another example: *I am destined, I believe in God's support, I commit to build altars to remember*.

Listen in prayer to see which ones the Holy Spirit might be leading you to focus on right now. Write them down and recite at least twice a day.

3. 30-day deep dive.

Some of these ideas and actions may require a major adjustment in your life. Be kind to yourself. You don't have to change everything overnight. In this practice, I suggest focusing in on one affirmation which seems the most difficult. For example: *I believe in God's timing* or *I commit to praying because my life depends on it*. For the next 30 days, pour all of your intention towards understanding this affirmation in a deeper way.

Read books on the subject. Ask your pastor or another mature Christian how they have come to trust in God's timing or the importance of prayer (or whatever your subject may be). Write about why you struggle to accept this truth compared to others. Also, write about the potential benefits to fully believing it and the downsides to not believing it. All the while reciting the troublesome affirmation at least one time per day.

What I have found through this exercise is that these *Magnetic Word* statements are linked in ways I couldn't have imagined. I might begin by thinking I have a problem committing to read my Bible when in reality I actually have a problem believing some core element of my identity in God. I guarantee you'll be surprised by what you find if you give yourself the grace and space to truly search.

I have not found a one-size-fits-all formula for integrating these magnetic words into every person's life. Each one of us begins somewhere unique. We have experiences and influences just like, and precisely unlike, any other human being. That means you must do the careful work of walking with Christ in truth and allowing His spirit to guide your mouth.

The encouraging part of this whole process is that God WANTS this for us. He wants our triangles to be renewed. He's zealous for us to receive the identities, beliefs, actions, and words that will unlock the best He has for us. And therefore, He is committed to helping us along this journey.

You are not alone.

Moving Beyond Magnetic Words

The goal of this entire book is to ignite the *Magnetic Faith* I know you are capable of. To accomplish this, I have spent time introducing you to the most important, most non-negotiable elements of the words which will help you get there. However, all of this is only the starting point.

These words are the foundation you can use to build whatever it is that God is leading you towards. But to go as far and build as high as He intends, you will likely need more, new, and different words. At the end of this book, there will be an extensive resource list which can guide you as you progress in your journey.

For now, I want to give you permission.

Permission to risk. Permission to search the Scriptures and find the treasure God has hidden for you. Permission to seek out wisdom and community and let yourself be led to new depths of love and charity, which will, in turn, inspire new words to come forth. Permission to be a fountain of encouragement to your brothers and sisters in Christ, especially to ones who are hurting or abandoned.

And finally, permission to speak your truest desires.

The level of satisfaction in your life will be determined by the content of your words. Life or death. Abundance or lack. God-led purpose or fear-led pain.

You (quite literally) have a say in the direction of your life. I pray you choose boldly.

How To Create and Control Your Words

Words are the binding force of your *Magnetic Faith*. Without them, the triangle falls apart. I've given you a number of lists and high-level actions throughout this book. Here I want to provide you with one more list specifically geared towards implementing what you have learned in the *Magnetic Words* portion, and how you can solidify the entire process of developing your faith now that you have all four parts.

1. **Reread the Series.** You probably thought that since you finished this book you were done with all the required reading…almost my friend! Have you experienced when you read a book or watch a movie the second time through, you catch things you didn't the first time around? It happens to me all of the time, and usually the gems I find the second or third time through are exactly the pieces I needed. My encouragement to you is to go and start back at *Magnetic Identity*

and read through the series now that you have the full picture in your mind. You will make connections you didn't know were there and progress much faster than if you just continued on with whatever you currently remember. Real change requires real commitment and I know you have it in you!

2. **Go on a Word Watch.** In some of the previous titles, we mentioned ways to inventory or catalog what you are already doing in terms of thoughts and actions. A word watch is the same concept but applied to our speech. Exactly how you implement this can vary but the main motivation is to increase your word awareness so that you can begin to make conscious changes.
    I. Commit to intentionally listening to your own words and the words of others for one full week.
    II. At the end of day one, take 5 minutes to sit in silence and review everything you said that day. Obviously, you won't remember everything, that's okay. You want to focus on the statements which bring about an emotional reaction. Did you gossip or yell? Did you encourage or validate? What words do you regret saying? What words do you wish you said? Simply review all of these in your mind and end by asking God to help you honor Him with your words tomorrow.
    III. Repeat this activity for 2 more days.

IV. At the end of day four, instead of reviewing your own words, take 5 minutes to review the words of others. Again, focus on the statements which evoke some kind of emotion in you. Were there words that hurt? Words that healed? What patterns could you identify with and what would you have said differently? The point of this exercise is not to judge these other people, but to examine what their words revealed about their hearts and how they impacted others. Remember, your words are also shaping the lives of others for better or worse.

V. Repeat this second activity for 2 more days.

VI. On day 7, write out in detail how you can bring more magnetic words into your daily speech, along with why you want to. This explanation is for your eyes only. I often find that there are thoughts behind my thoughts, but the only way to reach them is to let everything flow out onto a page. Write whatever you feel led and you will likely discover some powerful opportunities and reasons to reshape your speech.

3. **Read Scripture Aloud.** I never understood why it was so important to stretch before exercise until I started running regularly and developed

shin splints. If you've never had them (be grateful!), they are small micro tears that develop in the muscle on the front of your leg below the knee. They are relatively harmless in the long-term and can usually be prevented by a few simple stretches before exercise. Stretches prepare your body to receive the full benefit of the exercise you are about to put it through. Stretches get the blood flowing, loosen up any tightness which may have developed, and strengthens the connection between your body and mind.

In the same way, taking time to read the Bible out loud is like performing stretches for your *Magnetic Faith*. It prepares the mind, body, and soul. It loosens up any spiritual stiffness which may be sticking around and enables your *Magnetic Words* to have their full, intended effect. I would suggest beginning with the Psalms, but any of the poetic books or letters will get you started off on the right foot.

4. **Find a Partner.** One of the most beneficial practices I've come across when thinking about the power of words was one I accidentally stumbled into. My wife and I came up with seven affirmations we each wanted to stick with for an entire year. We printed them out, posted them on one of our bedroom walls, and read them aloud together every morning and every night. One night, I was exhausted from a particularly stressful day at work and didn't want to bother

reciting any affirmations. So my wife came over and started reciting them to me in "you" form. For example: *You believe in abundance. You are loved.*

It was the first time I had heard my personal affirmations come out of somebody else's mouth. It was a powerful moment. Not only did I recite my affirmations back to her (in the normal "I" form), we started implementing this back and forth method the very next day. She would say her words "I am..." and I would repeat back to her "You are...". I can't recommend this practice enough. Find a partner, whether it be a spouse or friend or mentor, and find a time for you both to confirm each other's affirmations.

Psalm 19:14 says, "May these words of my mouth and this meditation of my heart be pleasing in your sight, Lord, my Rock and my Redeemer." This is the goal of *Magnetic Words*, to put forth speech which God finds pleasing. To send out words like ambassadors for good. And to rejoice in the type of harvest they eventually bring. Your words are both the inciting action and the final product of your faith. Use them well, because you can be sure they will come back around to use you.

Closing

Congratulations on completing your journey through this *Magnetic Faith* volume! I hope you know how few people actually read a book in its entirety. So I know that by reaching this point, you are truly a rare individual who is willing to commit to whatever it takes.

In these four parts (Identity, Mindset, Habits, Words) I have attempted to give you everything you need to BEGIN your journey of life and faith transformation. For the most part, I learned these lessons the hard way. Through sacrifice, pain, and failure. My hope is that by laying them out for you in this book, you can reach even greater heights than me in a fraction of the time (and with an even smaller fraction of the frustration).

Implement the ideas found in this book and I promise you will experience a greater life than you thought possible. I can say that with bold confidence not because of what I can do, but on the firm foundation of what God can do...that is, if you ask Him.

So go! Ask. Risk. Build.

Discover who you really are, cultivate a brilliantly powerful mind, commit to the actions that will take you where you want to go, and transform your tongue into a fountain of blessing for both yourself and others.

It's time to activate your *Magnetic Faith*!

Recommended Reading List

Books listed in order by title. I have read each one at least once and received immense benefit from incorporating the ideas and practices contained within. Please note that this list contains a mixture of both Christian and secular titles, so make sure to read the descriptions of the book before purchasing to ensure it is appropriate for what you are seeking. Congratulations on taking your Magnetic Faith seriously!

You can find links directly to these titles here:
http://www.ramosauthor.com/blog/magnetic-faith-recommended-reading-list

About the Bible by Terence E. Fretheim

Atomic Habits by James Clear

Awaken the Giant Within by Tony Robbins

Battlefield of the Mind by Joyce Meyer

Born to Win by Zig Ziglar

Chase the Lion by Mark Batterson

Commit To Win by Heidi Reeder

Crowned with David by David Ramos

Essential Zen Habits by Leo Babauta

Girl, Wash Your Face by Rachel Hollis

God is Good by Bill Johnson

God's Creative Power for Finances by Charles Capps

Mindset by Carol Dweck

Poverty, Riches, and Wealth by Kris Vallotton

Power Words by Joyce Meyer

The 7 Habits That Will Change Your Life Forever by Adam Houge

The Miracle Morning by Hal Elrod

The Power of I Am by Joel Osteen

The Prayer of Jabez by Bruce Wilkinson

Thou Shall Prosper by Daniel Lapin

Unlimited Power by Tony Robbins

Vision to Reality by Honoree Corder

You Are a Badass by Jen Sincero

Magnetic Faith Mantra

When I accept the person God has destined me to be,

I will attract the things God has for me.

My identity produces my thoughts. As I think the thoughts God intends for my mind to think,

I will attract the things God has for me.

My thoughts produce my actions. As I boldly act in faith,

I will attract the things God has for me.

My words shape my life. As I speak truth,

I will attract the things God has for me.

About The Author

David Ramos is a Christian author and Bible teacher who is passionate about communicating the life-changing truths found in Scripture. He has a B.A. in Classical and Medieval Studies (like C.S. Lewis), an M.A. in Biblical Studies from Ashland Theological Seminary, and recently completed a Certificate of Theology from Princeton Theological Seminary. His goal is to educate others so that they may serve God to greater heights by seeking Him to greater depths.

Over the last 5 years David has published over 1,000,000 words across nearly 100 publications and blogs. His books (12+) have reached over 250,000 readers and garnered invitations to speak at churches and universities across the country.

Learn more at RamosAuthor.com.

More Books by David Ramos

Climbing with Abraham: 30 Devotionals to Help You Grow Your Faith, Build Your Life, and Discover God's Calling

Chosen with Esther: 20 Devotionals to Awaken Your Calling, Guide Your Heart, and Empower You To Lead By God's Design

Daring with Ruth: 18 Devotionals to Ignite Your Courage, Transform Your Hope, and Reveal God's True Character

Crowned with David: 40 Devotionals to Inspire Your Life, Fuel Your Trust, and Help You Succeed in God's Way

Enduring with Job: 30 Devotionals to Give You Hope, Stir Your Faith, and Find God's Power in Your Pain

Escaping with Jacob: 30 Devotionals to Help You Find Your Identity, Forgive Your Past, and Walk in Your Purpose

The God with a Plan

What The Bible Says About Purpose

I Need Your Help!

Writing is both my personal calling and the tool I use to help others fulfill their own callings. God intended it to work that way. For us, the body, to rely on one another to see our callings come to fruition. Hopefully, the few words God has given me can help you on your journey. And right now, your words can also help me on my journey.

Please take a minute to write a short review for this book on Amazon. These reviews are a tremendous help – every single one expands the ministry God has given me to shepherd. I know your time is precious and so I am deeply grateful for your review.

Thank you!

-David

[i] https://www.etymonline.com/word/freedom
[ii] https://www.etymonline.com/word/free
[iii] http://www.slate.com/articles/health_and_science/elements/features/2010/blogging_the_periodic_table/aluminum_it_used_to_be_more_precious_than_gold.html
[iv] Crowned With David. http://a.co/d/3ojQlgW
[v] Is there enough oxygen for a growing population? http://www.greenlineprint.com/blog/is-there-enough-oxygen-for-a-growing-population
[vi] https://en.wikipedia.org/wiki/Framing_effect_(psychology)
[vii] https://www.oneyoufeed.net/tale-of-two-wolves/
[viii] https://www.etymonline.com/word/expect
[ix] https://en.wikipedia.org/wiki/Endorheic_basin
[x] https://hbr.org/2012/06/habits-why-we-do-what-we-do
[xi] 1 Samuel 15:22
[xii] If you want to learn my exact method for studying the Bible, I encourage you to join the following course: https://faithspring.teachable.com/p/7-pillars-bible-study
[xiii] You can read the full story here: http://a.co/d/aEsOoyP
[xiv] https://www.biblestudytools.com/dictionary/altar/
[xv] https://en.wikipedia.org/wiki/Form_follows_function
[xvi] https://zenhabits.net/habitses/
[xvii] How many words are there in the English language? https://en.oxforddictionaries.com/explore/how-many-words-are-there-in-the-english-language/
[xviii] Dikaiosuné definition: https://biblehub.com/greek/1343.htm
[xix] How commitment shapes our lives by Heidi Reeder: https://www.youtube.com/watch?v=lKE_ebex2tk

Made in the USA
Columbia, SC
31 October 2020